Graphic Design:
America

Rockport Allworth *Editions*
Ten East Twenty-third Street
New York, New York
10010

. Copublishers:
Rockport Publishers, Inc.
Allworth Press

Rockport**Allworth***Editions*

November 20, 1993

Mr. Fred Seibert, President
Hanna Barbera
3400 Cahuenga Blvd.
Hollywood, CA 90068

Dear Fred Seibert,

Twenty - eight graphic design firms from across North America were selected to represent the emerging spirit of graphic design at the time when graphic design has truly come of age. The result is *Graphic Design: America*.

Besides being a valuable reference work, *Graphic Design: America* is, in a sense, a time capsule. And, like all effective time capsules, it's not just what you put in it but where you deposit it that counts.

It is, therefore, at the suggestion of one of the book's participants, Charles S. Anderson, that we are presenting you a copy of *Graphic Design: America* for your library.

Unlike a time capsule, we hope you'll open it soon and often.

Best regards,

DK Holland   Michael Bierut   William Drenttel

Lewin/Holland, Inc.   Pentagram Design   Drenttel Doyle Partners

Enc. *Graphic Design: America*
CC: Charles S. Anderson, Charles S. Anderson Design Co.

Graphic Design: America

The work of twenty-eight
leading-edge design firms from
across the United States and Canada

Organized by
DK Holland
Michael Bierut and
William Drenttel

Introduction by
Stephen Heller

Essays by
William Drenttel
Jennifer Morla
Forrest & Valerie Richardson
and Rick Valicenti

Designed by
Pentagram

Published by
Rockport/Allworth Editions
Rockport Publishers, Inc.
Allworth Press

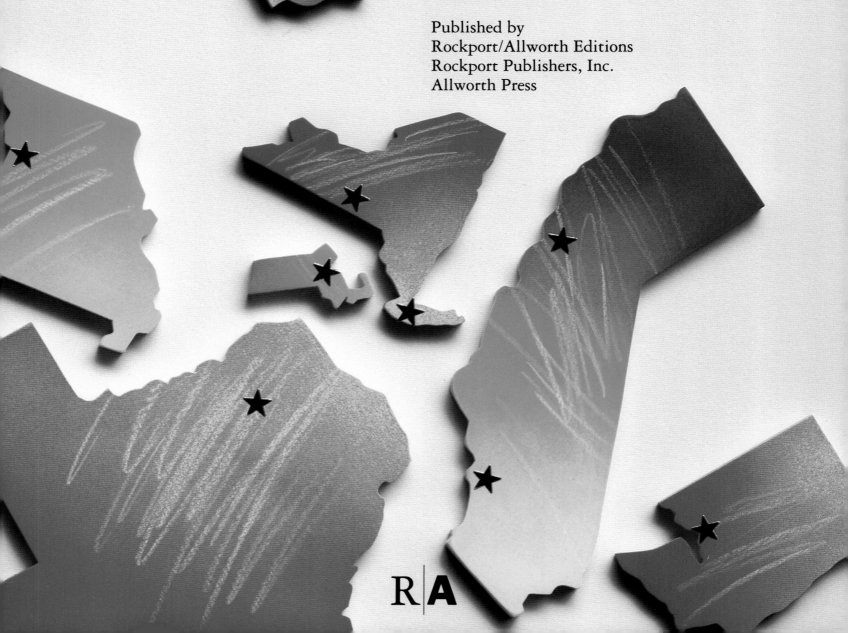

R|A

First published in the
United States by
Rockport Allworth
Editions, a trade name of
Rockport Publishers,
Inc. and Allworth Press.

Rockport Publishers, Inc.
146 Granite Street
Rockport, Massachusetts
01966
Telephone:
508/546-9590
Fascimile:
508/546-7141
Telex: 5186019284
ROCKPORT PUB

Allworth Press
10 East 23rd Street
New York, NY 10010
Telephone:
212/777-8395
Fascimile:
212/777-8261

Project Director:
DK Holland,
Lewin/Holland, Inc.
Book Designer:
Michael Bierut,
Pentagram
Writer:
Steven Heller
Copy Editor:
Philip F. Clark
Project Manager:
Lisa Cerveny
Assistant Project
Manager:
Esther Bridavsky
Production:
Lisette Buiani
Printer:
Regent, Hong Kong

Distribution to the book
trade and art trade in
the United States and
Canada by:
North Light Books,
an imprint of:
F&W Publications
1507 Dalton Avenue
Cincinnati, Ohio 45207
Telephone:
513/531-2222

Distributed to book
trade and art trade
throughout the rest of
the world by:
Rockport Publishers, Inc.
Rockport, Massachusetts
01966

ISBN: 1-56496-030-7
Printed in Hong Kong

Table of Contents

6

Acknowledgements

Almost three years ago, Tad Crawford of Allworth Press had the idea of creating *Graphic Design: New York*, a firm-by-firm survey of Manhattan's top design organizations. The success of that book led us to extend the concept to up-and-coming design firms across the country in this volume. Once again, Tad invited Rockport Publishers to join the project as co-publishers. Rockport's Stan Patey, Don Traynor and Marta Scooler lent their invaluable publishing and sales expertise and wisdom throughout the project.

Putting together a book like this one is by necessity a team effort. Many people worked long and hard to make *Graphic Design: America* a reality.

On the editorial front, the three of us and Tad Crawford formed a committee to usher *Graphic Design: America* through all its phases of production. We are indebted to the book's writer, the tireless Steven Heller who became like a fourth partner. Besides advise and counsel, he provided an essay that articulates his views on graphic design in America at the end of the century, and for overseeing the introductory copy for each firm. Philip Clark, our able copy editor, worked relentlessly against impossible deadlines. E.J. Gallegos of Lewin/Holland, Inc. ran interference whenever communications looked like they might get bogged down, keeping lines open with the 28 firms in the book.

Pentagram's Lisa Cerveny and Esther Bridavsky coordinated the book's complex production process with their characteristic good humor and dedication. Lisette Buiani produced (and revised, and revised) *Graphic Design: America*'s mechanical artwork on an Apple II in Quark Xpress. To keep up with the book's hectic schedule, Lisette got some help along the way from Erin Van Slyke. Typogram provided final camera-ready output with their usual high level of professional expertise. Finally, Regent Printing artfully placed ink on paper, making the whole process worthwhile.

Finally and naturally, our greatest thanks go to the 28 firms who had the confidence that we could collectively pull this off. From New York City to Nome, Alaska, graphic design is rapidly becoming a household word. It's the passion, professionalism and dedication of graphic designers like those featured in this book that is transforming the way our country communicates in the nineties.

DK Holland
Michael Bierut
William Drenttel
New York

About This Book

Graphic Design is the art of the people. Packages are seen on grocery store shelves, books in bookstores, images on computer screens, and titles begin and end all motion pictures. All designed by a graphic designer. Most people know the words "graphic design," yet few can define what they mean.

Choosing the firms to be invited into the book was, in one way, very difficult, in another very easy. None of us had seen the entire portfolio of many of the firms that were asked; that made it hard to "see" what the book would look like. We were concerned with the book's integrity and balance, and wanted to represent graphic design in America equally, yet we realized that such a book easily could be the size of the *Encyclopedia Brittanica*. So we took pains to search for a select group of worthy designers to reflect a broad philosophical and geographic mix, focusing primarily on new designers and favoring designers whose work is created for a variety of clients.

We sought to achieve a sense of discovery. Many worthy firms didn't make the invitation list because they were too established and well known. We see *Graphic Design: America* as a publicity collective. Each of the 28 firms or individuals included were asked to create a portfolio for the reader of their body of work, and to defray some of the publication expenses.

Graphic Design: America has been very rewarding on many levels, not the least has been the chance to express the vitality of design in America.

DK Holland
Michael Bierut
William Drenttel
New York City
September, 1992

HOW to BECOME an ARTIST Designer Illustrator Cartoonist

WASHINGTON SCHOOL
of ART INC.
Washington, D.C.

Steven Heller, a senior
art director of *The New
York Times*, teaches
The History of Visual
Communications at the
School of Visual Arts
MFA/Illustration
program. His over
twenty books include:
*Man Bites Man:
Two Decades of Satiric
Art 1960-80; Innovators
of American Illustration;
Low Budget
High/Quality Design;
Graphic Wit: The Art of
Humor in Design; The
Savage Mirror:
The Art of Contemporary
Caricature; Art Against
War; Art of New York;
Graphic Style: From
Victorian to Post Modern*;
and *Borrowed Design: Use
and Abuse of Historical
Form*. He is the editor
of *The AIGA Journal of
Graphic Design*, and
with Seymour Chwast
is co-director of Push
Pin Editions.

State of The Union: American Design and Designers

Steven Heller

Who would have thunk?" is neither
an astute nor acerbic way to
begin an analysis of the current
state of North American graphic
design, however, it is an apt
response to the diversification, eclecticization, and, at
various times, anarchicization of American graphic
design practice during the past fifteen years. This was
a period of reevaluation which began in the mid-1970s
when "post" prefixed modern; layering replaced
simplicity; zigguarats, lozenges, leaderdots and
sawtooth rules suddenly appeared; and a tide of stylis-
tic waves—new and old—ebbed and flowed. It's
also an incredulous response to the unprecedented,
widespread acceptance of graphic design as a full-
fledged profession when, owing to economic, cultural,
and social phenomena, a relatively arcane practice
was catapulted into the public's consciousness.

The late 1970s and early 1980s
saw the democraticization—and the regionalization—
of graphic design. Almost overnight visual communications became a viable business for many
who had never considered it before. Nevermind that
the field is not recognized by the United States
Department of Labor—which has lumped it together
with other design categories, including flower
arranging—a record number of students and other
career-bound people have chosen to practice
graphic design anyway. An unprecedented rise across
the continent of privately owned design studios,
offices, and firms has shifted the demographics from
the principal American media centers, New York,
Chicago, Los Angeles, and San Francisco to industrial
regions throughout the Northwest, Northeast,
Midwest, Southwest, Southeast and Canada. Based
on the growth of the American Institute of Graphic
Arts' chapters in 35 states the population of
graphic designers throughout the nation has increased
many fold during the course of a decade.

Who would have predicted fifteen years ago that the AIGA, the benchmark of American graphic design activity, would grow from around 1000 members in the late 1970s to 7000 members today? In fact, this figure is merely the tip of the iceberg; no one knows exactly, not least of all this premier organization, how many graphic designers are currently working in the various disciplines now under the graphic design or visual communications umbrella. However, the field's leading trade periodicals, *Print* and *Communication Arts*, each sell an average of 50,000 copies per issue, which is meager compared to most national magazines, but impressive when stacked up to the considerably smaller circulation figures of ten years ago. Considering the addition in the mid-1980s of two more competitive publications, *How* and *Step-by-Step* it must be assumed that graphic design is a healthy (and potentially wealthy) field to be able to support these and other trade journals. But even more conclusive evidence is the large amount of high quality work regularly showcased in these magazines. Each year an increasing number of young designers prove themselves worthy of national attention.

Subway signage
standards manual for
New York City
Transit Authority,
1966. Designer,
Massimo Vignelli,
Unimark International.
▲

Signage for children's
store Heffalump, 1985.
Designer, Michael
Manwaring, The Office
of Michael Manwaring.
▲

The reasons for the current popularity of graphic design are varied. One theory says that careers in the fine arts are so impractical these days (as if they ever were really practical) that more realistic financial priorities have contributed to an increased number of students entering graphic design rather than fine arts programs in colleges and art schools. Indeed graphic design offers some of the creative perquisites of the fine arts with the promise of a steady income, too. More revealing, though, is that the current surge in graphic design awareness began during Ronald Reagan's presidency (1980-88), a time when mainstream businesses were encouraged to expand, and prosperity flourished within certain, industrial regions of the country. That many new graphic design firms opened in close proximity to the new economic centers was consistent with the emergence of other support industries. In the Southwest, for example, the meteoric rise of oil profits in the mid-eighties contributed to a healthy real estate market, which in turn provided graphic designers with lucrative new outlets for their skills. Elsewhere in the country, where graphic design was at best a cottage industry, real estate speculators, financial institutions, high tech corporations, and other ostensibly conservative businesses became wellsprings for a fair amount of high budget and high quality design. Prior to this present era of enlightened clients a significant number of businesses established in the post-war period were using sophisticated graphic design to communicate corporate identity and philosophy. As some early design-conscious companies became more selfconfident about their images they also became relatively more adventuresome. Influenced by the few pioneers who made inroads in corporate design during the sixties and early seventies, a new generation of designers attempted to push the canonical limits and rules at such institutions as IBM, Container Corporation, Herman Miller, and others, and in some cases developed unprecedented graphic approaches and styles. Concurrently, a broader concept of design was mainstreamed into American culture through general design and lifestyle publications which promoted all kinds of design which swept graphic design along with it. Graphic design was, moreover, newly discovered by those who realized its value as a sales tool for business, as well as those who understood its broader cultural significance.

Recalling the 1920s when good design was honestly seen as a cure for the world's economic and social ills, in the eighties design was increasingly used, with less utopian commitment, to cover up the world's blemishes. Design became panacea. At once, used to heighten aesthetic standards and make products more marketable. Advertisers touted designer-made products, and designer imprints on everything from softdrinks to automobiles became signs of virtue. Yet in the final analysis, much of the design was merely style, style equalled status, and graphic design, which has historically been both an organizing tool and an aesthetic veneer, became a means by which codes were developed for communicating degrees of status.

Graphic design awareness was at its zenith in the eighties among certain influential businesses, most notably those concerned with fashion, food, (clothing, accessories, furniture), as well as food and sundries for whom allure (or appetite appeal) is the key to success. No wonder graphic designers who traded in fashionable styles did well in this receptive environment. The thousands of entries to the AIGA Communication

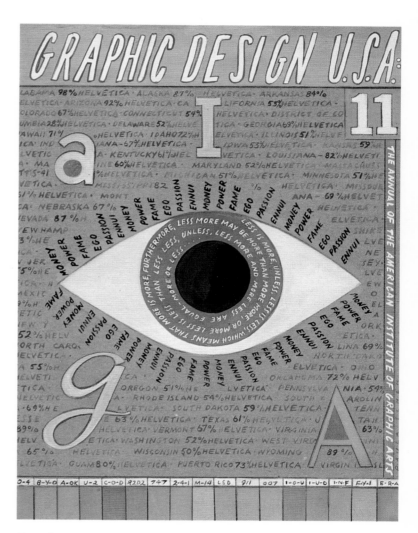

Cover for *AIGA Graphic Design: USA*, 1990. Designer, Paula Scher, Koppel and Scher.
▲

"Get out the vote"
posters, 1976.
Designer, Wilburn
Bonnell, Container
Corporation of America.

▲

Graphic design shows of the eighties prove that enthusiastic clients with generous budgets were the rule, not the exception. However, the best graphic designers were not simply stylists or makers of pleasing veneers, but more often than not, developed ambitious marketing strategies and campaigns. During the eighties being in the visual communications business implied having more than just good typographic or drawing skills, it signified an ability to integrate graphic style, marketing know-how, and packaging expertise into a single service, similar to the role of the traditional advertising agency. In fact, graphic design steadily grew as a profession because the truly "enlightened" client embraced the truly savvy graphic designer as a partner in business, not a glorified layout artist.

Although close collaborations between designers and clients were not new to the eighties—the pioneers of modern design in the late thirties and forties were able to get their untraditional approaches accepted through the support, if not friendship of the chief decision makers of the businesses which they serviced—this special relationship began to change after World War II when major corporations began to expand. As a result hierarchical layers included middle management personnel responsible for communications but answerable to committees and boards; designers soon found it hard to sell their ideas free from committee interference. Some designers left the field, others strengthened their management ties, and many simply adapted to the new rules. Without overly simplifying the business conditions contributing to standardization and professionalization of graphic design, it can be said that the need for design on a corporate level gave rise to large, impersonal firms that practiced an "international style," such as Lippincott and Marguiles and Landor Associates in whose hands design was rooted in research and resulted in formulas. Inevitably, this fostered a reaction by smaller studios that practiced a variety of eclectic approaches, such as Push Pin Studios, whose ethic was to liven up the world by combining nostalgic, vernacular, and contemporary aesthetics in all their graphic work.

The practice of North American graphic design today has more or less developed from the healthy tension between Modernism and Eclecticism of the late 1950s and early 1960s. Today design can be rational and functional, personal and eccentric, experimental and avant garde. During the 1980s an increase in comparatively small entrepreneurial businesses in atypical areas around the country allowed designers to once again work directly with the chief proprietors. Designers who veered from the expected and accepted were welcomed by those businesses whose identities were enhanced by idiosyncratic design. In a market that was consuming more and more design the more idiosyncracy the better, and the license afforded a few eventually became the norm for many. The relaxation of strictures within the business world is not the only genesis of the expressive and raucous contemporary graphic design practiced today. The personal computer has contributed to a lot of the controlled chaos that characterizes eighties design. The Macintosh, which was introduced at the same time that other seductive multimedia inventions were causing graphic designers to approach the visual language from different perspectives, made the process of design more accessible to more people than ever before. For many young graphic designers their first introduction to the field might have been the "infamous" 1985 Apple Computer television commercial in which the public was introduced to what graphic designers do, and were also told that with the new Macintosh (desktop publishing system) anyone can do the same job. Despite its negative connotations, the computer inspired many young people to explore graphic design as a viable profession.

Who would have predicted in the mid-1970s, when photocomposition finally won the battle for dominance as the typographic state of the art, that only a few years later a new technology would literally revolutionize the process, if not the fundamental practice of graphic design? It's hard to believe, as many forward-thinkers are now asserting, that with continued progress in hypertext and hypermedia graphic design as it's currently practiced will radically change, and perhaps by the year 2000 the term graphic design may no longer be an adequate one. Whatever the future holds, many

Pushpinoff candies packaging, 1980. Designer, Seymour Chwast, The Pushpin Group.
▲

Product packaging for Mobil, 1975. Tom Geismar, Chermayeff & Geismar Inc.
▲

celebrate the time saving advancements brought about by the computer yet condemn the debasements that these pyrotechnics have wrought. Nevertheless, and perhaps for this reason, contemporary graphic design, as practiced by the new generation of designers, is compelling and controversial.

Virtually the same friction causing controversy among graphic designers today existed fifty years ago when Modernists threatened to dismantle the antiquated practices of their era. Yet today a variety of public forums (conferences, special interest groups, publications, and so on) effectively publicize these issues on a grander scale than ever before. The design literature from the 1930s documents outspoken critics such as T.M. Cleland, who called one of his anti-Modernist speeches "Harsh Words," or W.A. Dwiggins, who referred in an essay to the Modernists as "those Bauhaus boys," taking frequent jabs at designers whose experiments were jaundicely viewed as fashionable and superficial. While "fashionable" was sometimes a buzzword for new and threatening, it could sometimes be an accurate assessment of malpractice resulting from the following of popular trends. Today's critics argue against the same basic issues: legibility versus illegibility, ornamentation versus functionalism, and so on, and present a valid case when applied to the worst abuses.

The computer has made it easier to achieve radical and ridiculous concoctions, however, the reasons for pushing the envelope are basically the same as always throughout history. Stretching the bounds of convention and rebelling against tradition are the motives; and the results include both forgettable attempts, as well as welcome new paradigms. Despite the complaints by the critics who rail against excess layering, deconstructivist typography, vernacular revival, and the rest of design's *betes noir* of the eighties and nineties, constant movement, even if the results are abominable, is better than accepting the canon at face value. Milton Glaser wisely points out that "everybody must make their own discoveries, even if they are old discoveries."

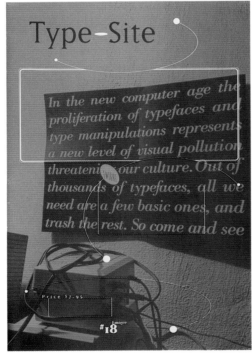

"Graphic Design in America" billboard for the Walker Art Center, 1990. Designer, April Greiman, April Greiman Associates.
▲

Cover for *Emigre* magazine, Issue No. 18, 1991. Designer, Rudy Vanderlans, Emigre Graphics.
▲

The work which appears in *Graphic Design: America* represents a generation of designers who, for the most part, began their individual practices in the early 1980s, were introduced to the field before computers (BC) yet matured during the computer age (CA). For some this technology has greatly influenced their graphic style, for others the results are invisible. These designers represent a wide range of approaches—from traditional to experimental, functional to decorative. Some are deliberately, even selfconsciously, unconventional, others have reinterpreted convention to suit specific personal or business requirements. Wit and humor are common to all, while standards of beauty and elegance vary considerably. Yet all have wed the requisites of business with the passions of art to create distinctive identities, if not exclusively for their clients, then for themselves.

Because this century's major aesthetic and ideological battles were fought by previous generations, these designers are not apt to be rigidly Modern or Post-Modern; indeed adhering to "isms" is not a major issue. Rather, the designers represented here suggest that anything is possible: stasis or change, evolution or revolution. Despite flirtations with semantics, linguistics, and New Age theory born of academic nearsightedness, the majority of designers here simply practice the art and business of graphic design without conceit; they appear to perform it effectively in a field with fewer constraints than that of previous generations who were constricted by geography, technology, and a limited universe of enlightened clients. Who would have predicted thirty, twenty, even fifteen years ago that the future of North American graphic design would be built upon such remarkable diversity? The changes in the field over the past fifteen years have occurred so fast and have been so consequential that, analysis aside, it begs the question: "Who would have thunk?"

"Flirting With the Edge" poster for the American Center for Design, 1992. Designer, Barry Deck.
▼

"Live to Death" poster, student project at Cranbrook Academy of Art, 1991. Designer, P. Scott Makela.
▼

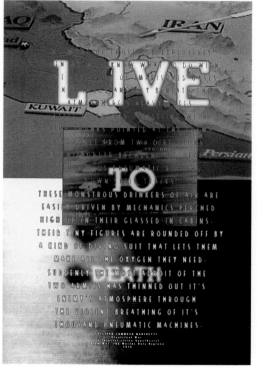

**Charles S. Anderson
Design Company**

Thirty North First Street
Minneapolis, MN 55401
612/339-5181

From left to right:
Ricé Davis, Charles S.
Anderson, Lisa Pemrick,
Todd Hauswirth;
Photographer, Paul
Irmiter.
▼

Nike 180 Air, poster
design introducing the
newest air technology
shoe, for Weiden &
Kennedy Advertising,
Portland, Oregon. Art
Director, Charles S.
Anderson; Designers,
Daniel Olson, Charles S.
Anderson, Haley Johnson;
Production Artist,
Randall Dahlk.
▲

Metal "Book Shelf" file for
the Charles S. Anderson
Design Company. The
file makes it easy for
clients to keep a portfolio
of the designers' work
on hand. Art Director,
Charles S. Anderson;
Designers, Charles S.
Anderson, Daniel Olson;
Copywriter, Lisa Pemrick;
Production Artist, Randall
Dahlk.
▶

Poster design for the
Dallas Society of Visual
Communications, Dallas,
Texas. The poster was
printed in 4/C on
French Speckletone
using dryography for
a 3-D effect. Designers,
Charles S. Anderson,
Daniel Olson, Todd
Hauswirth; Art Director,
Charles S. Anderson;
Copywriter, Lisa Pemrick;
Production Artist,
Randall Dahlk.
▼

Principals:
Charles S. Anderson
Year Founded: 1989
Size of Firm: 5
Key Clients:
Adobe Systems,
Distillerie des Aravis,
El Paso Chile Company,
Fossil Watch Company,
The French Paper
Company,
Levis,
Nike,
Pantone, Inc.,
Paramount Pictures,
Ralph Lauren

Charles S. Anderson Design Company

A s Americans are bombarded by more and more images, advertisements and messages with less and less time to read them, the Charles S. Anderson Design Company has responded with a very simple answer: simple intuitive design that cuts through the slick, high-tech clutter. Their work reflects the optimism of technology with a friendly, hand-made look that is applied to product design, identity and packaging. Currently they are developing a line of home furnishings and other products through a licensing agreement with Paramount Pictures. When asked about their philosophy, Anderson asserts, "We have no desire to be the biggest or the richest design firm on the planet. Basically, we re in it for the craft... the artistic quality of the finished product is always our top priority."

Charles S. Anderson
Company project
cards are an expandable
series that documents
the firm's work. Art
Director, Charles S.
Anderson; Designers,
Charles S. Anderson,
Daniel Olson; Copywriter,
Lisa Pemrick; Production
Artist, Randall Dahlk;
Typography, Todd
Hauswirth.
◄

One of a series of three posters designed to promote Pantone's dominant position in the graphic arts. Art Director, Designer, and Illustrator, Charles S. Anderson.
▼

Barber Ellis Grade Report brochure spread, for the French Paper Company, Niles, Michigan. Designed in the shape and format of a school themebook, the cover and copy carry the theme of "grading" from "A" to "F" for "Don't Fail to Come." Art Director, Charles S. Anderson; Designers, Charles S. Anderson, Daniel Olson; Copy-writer, Lisa Pemrick; Production Artist, Randall Dahlk.
▼

Stationery system designed for Minneapolis College of Art & Design, Minneapolis, Minnesota. Art Director, Charles S. Anderson; Designers, Charles S. Anderson, Daniel Olson; Production Artist, Randall Dahlk.
▶

"How To Keep Romance From Losing Its Luster," promotional book for Pantone, Inc., Moonachie, New Jersey. Art Director, Charles S. Anderson; Designers, Charles S. Anderson, Daniel Olson, Haley Johnson; Copy-writer, Lisa Pemrick; Production Artist, Randall Dahlk.
▼

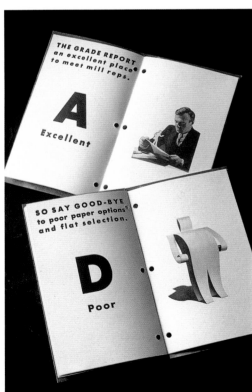

Identity and vehicle application for Print Craft, Inc., St. Paul, Minnesota. The 11-ft. high logo was intentionally designed to be so loud and overpowering that you had to notice it. Art Director, Charles S. Anderson; Designers, Charles S. Anderson, Daniel Olson; Production Artist, Randall Dahlk.
◄

Sample swatchbooks designed for the French Paper Company, Niles, Michigan. The unique format saves 50% of the paper normally used for these products. Art Directors and Designers, Charles S. Anderson, Daniel Olson; Illustrators, Haley Johnson, Charles S. Anderson, Randall Dahlk; Copywriter, Lisa Pemrick; Production Artist, Randall Dahlk.
▼

Poster designed to introduce a new line of four industrial-grade printing papers. Art Director, Charles S. Anderson; Designers, Charles S. Anderson, Todd Hauswirth; Copywriter, Lisa Pemrick.
▼

Cover design for *Design Typography*, featuring a series of wood block make-readies printed by Hatch Show Print of Nashville, TN in the '30's, '40's and '50's. Art Director, Charles S. Anderson; Designers, Charles S. Anderson, Todd Hauswirth; Copywriter, Lisa Pemrick.
▲

Charles S. Anderson Design Company

Bedding designs for Paramount Products, Hollywood, California. The design features theatrical iconography. Art Director, Charles S. Anderson; Designer and Illustrator, Haley Johnson; Production Artist, Randall Dahlk. ▼

Hollywood alarm clock for Paramount Products, Hollywood, California evokes the dusty time-pieces uncovered in the Paramount prop rooms. Art Director, Charles S. Anderson; Designers, Daniel Olson, Charles S. Anderson; Production Artist, Randall Dahlk. ▶

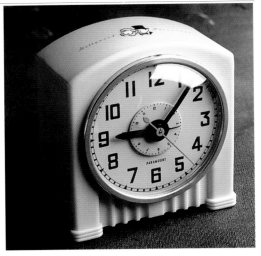

Brochure design for Paramount Pictures, Hollywood, California. The brochure documents the history, glamour, and magic of Paramount and Hollywood in its heydey. Art Director, Charles S. Anderson; Designers, Charles S. Anderson, Daniel Olson; Copywriter, Lisa Pemrick; Production Artist, Randall Dahlk; Illustrator, Haley Johnson; Photography, Lennon, Bausman & Fitzgerald.
▼

Formal dinnerware designs for Paramount Products, Hollywood, California. The design recreates settings that would have looked at home on any Hollywood table in the Thirties. Art Director, Charles S. Anderson; Designer, Haley Johnson; Production Artist, Randall Dahlk.
▼

Boy's clothing hang tag design for Polo Ralph Lauren, New York, New York. Each of the series of 12 tags highlights a sporting event with an embossed figure. Art Director, Charles S. Anderson; Designers, Daniel Olson, Charles S. Anderson; Copywriter, Lisa Pemrick; Production Artist, Randall Dahlk.
▼

**Charles S. Anderson
Design Company**

La Parisienne pear liqueur label design for Distillerie de Aravis, La Clusaz, France. The series of designs was based on the antique French postage stamp, to reflect the heritage of this 200-year-old distillery. The pear shown here is actually grown into the bottle on the tree. Art Director, Charles S. Anderson; Designers, Daniel Olson, Charles S. Anderson; Production Artist, Randall Dahlk.
▼

Poster to announce a speaking engagement for AIGA-L.A., using L.A.-related imagery such as sun, earthquakes and smog. Art Director, Charles S. Anderson; Designers, Charles S. Anderson, Todd Hauswirth; Copywriter, Lisa Pemrick.
▲

Desert Pepper Trading Company salsa label designs for the El Paso Chile Company, El Paso, Texas. Art Directors and Designers, Charles S. Anderson, Daniel Olson; Illustrators, Charles S. Anderson, Randall Dahlk; Copywriter, Lisa Pemrick; Production Artist, Randall Dahlk.
▲

Fossil watch tins for Overseas Products International, Inc. Four from a series of 16 silkscreened tin boxes for the Fossil Watch Company, Dallas, Texas. Each tin design is a limited edition, making them as collectible as the watches. Art Director, Charles S. Anderson; Designers, Charles S. Anderson, Daniel Olson, Haley Johnson; Copywriter, Lisa Pemrick; Production Artist, Randall Dahlk.
▼

New York Minute watch was designed as part of a joint venture between the designer and Fossil Watch Company. Tiny icons circling the face depict the average New York minute: a shooting, a run-in with a sewer rat, etc. Art Director, Charles S. Anderson; Designer, Charles S. Anderson; Production Artist, Randall Dahlk; Copywriter, Lisa Pemrick.
▼

Candy bar package designs for Cloud Nine, Inc., Hoboken, New Jersey. The packaging for these 100% natural gourmet chocolates is both recycled and recyclable. Art Director, Haley Johnson; Designer, Haley Johnson; Copywriter, Lisa Pemrick; Production Artist, Randall Dahlk.
▼

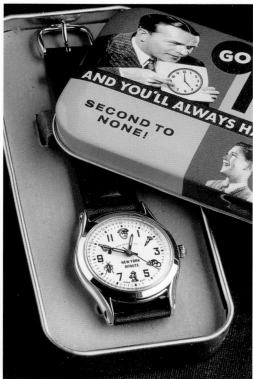

Truck Design for the St. Paul based printer, Litho, Inc., featuring their new identity. Reflective printers registration marks were applied to five sides of their bright orange delivery truck to create a traffic hazard both day and night. Art Director, Charles S. Anderson; Designers, Charles S. Anderson, Todd Hauswirth, Daniel Olson; Copywriter, Lisa Pemrick.
◀

Concrete

633 South Plymouth Ct.
Suite 208
Chicago, IL 60605
312/427-3733

Jilly Simons, principal
of Concrete; Photog-
rapher, François Robert.
▲

"Dance Party" invitation
for the 1991 American
Institute of Graphic
Arts (AIGA) National
Conference. Designers,
Jilly Simons, Cindy
Chang.
▶

Concrete brochure
espouses a hard-working
philosophy in a numbered
limited edition. Concrete
block promotion adds
weight to the company
name. "Over My Head"
poster playfully expresses
the serious roles of fear
and risk in the creative
process. Designers, Jilly
Simons, David Robson;
Copywriter, Deborah
Barron; Photographers,
Geof Kern (brochure),
François Robert (poster).
◀ ▲ ▶

Principal:
Jilly Simons
Year Founded: 1987
Size of Firm: 4 1/2
Key Clients:
American Bar
Association,
Arthur Andersen,
Blackbook Marketing
Group,
Diamond Headache
Clinic,
DIFFA/Chicago,
The Federal Reserve
Bank of Chicago,
Founders Financial
Corporation,
The Founders National
Trust Bank,
Christopher Hawker
Photography,
Homart,
Homart Community
Centers,
Mohawk Paper Mills,
Nottage & Ward,
Refco Group, Ltd.,
Tony Stone Worldwide,
United Stationers,
University of Chicago
Medical Center,
Wheeler Kearns
Architects

Concrete

OVER MY HEAD

DO YOU READ ME>OVER
OVER MY HEAD

Concrete principal Jilly Simons insists on simplicity in design and in the way it is produced. Simons' philosophy reflects her belief that "limits stimulate." Concrete's design solutions, however, are anything but limited in their passion and imagination. Born in the concrete jungle of New York, and raised in dissonant South Africa, Simons founded Concrete in 1987. Immediately her office began to build a solid body of work (and an impressive client portfolio) that has been published, awarded and exhibited extensively throughout the U.S. and internationally. Concrete's work, though conceptually complex, evolves seamlessly into pieces that are graphically unfussy and have a signature elegance of execution. The foundation of this work is communication, and that communication resonates.

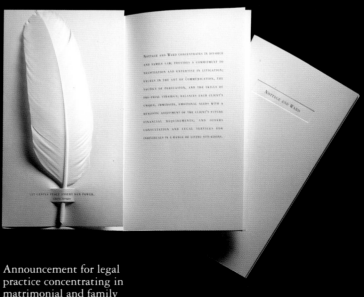

Announcement for legal practice concentrating in matrimonial and family law. Judicious use of language, imagery, and materials communicates the firm's sensitivity to the individual needs of their clients. Designers, Jilly Simons, David Robson; Copywriter, Deborah Barron.

▲

Corporate identity system for Florabunda. The client specializes in the design and planting of urban and contained gardens. Five marks were created, each incorporating various elements of planting and plant mythology. Designers, Jilly Simons, David Robson.
▼

Concrete

Series of covers and editorial spreads from *Reserve*/7, a quarterly publication of The Federal Reserve Bank of Chicago. Designers, Jilly Simons, David Robson, Cindy Chang. Photographers and Illustrator, Kevin Anderson, Pierre-Yves Goavec, Tim Lewis.
▼ ▶

Corporate identity for Triangle Ranch, a private club in Montana in which membership includes part ownership of four hundred acres of mountain valley. Designers, Jilly Simons, David Robson.
▲

Concrete

Corporate identity for Insurance Knowledge, Inc. Designers, Jilly Simons, David Robson.
▶

LIKE THE TORTOISE AND

THE HARE, EVOLUTION

AND REVOLUTION BOTH

SEEK THE SAME GOAL.

EVOLUTION, AS THE

TORTOISE, PROCEEDS

SLOWLY AND SURELY.

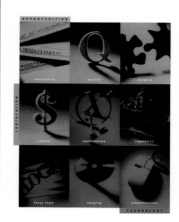

THE MATURATION OF TECHNOLOGY,

THE IMPACT OF NEW LEGISLATION,

THE MYRIAD BUSINESS OPPORTUNITIES

IN CHECK PROCESSING:

These are some of the issues shaping the Federal Reserve

Bank of Chicago in the 1990s.

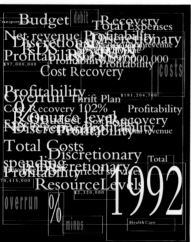

JUNE, 1991. THE LATEST EXPENSE RESULTS

SHOWED THE BANK TO BE $1.15 MILLION

OVER PLAN. *It looked like the Seventh District might not*

meet its year-end commitment. Something had to be done.

ON FEBRUARY FIFTH, TREASURY SECRETARY

NICHOLAS BRADY PRESENTED THE LONG

AND MUCH AWAITED BUSH ADMINISTRATION

PROPOSAL FOR THE FINANCIAL INDUSTRY

RESTRUCTURING. THE PROPOSAL, ENTITLED

"MODERNIZING THE FINANCIAL SYSTEM"

embodies many of the ideas of the prior Bush task force, headed

by the then vice president during the Reagan administration.

"Timesavers" identity for the American Bar Association was developed as a quick reference icon identifying publications in their catalog that contained useful time management information for attorneys. Designers, Jilly Simons, David Robson.
▶

Capabilities brochure for Refco Group, Ltd., one of the world's largest risk management firms. Designer, Jilly Simons. ▼

Corporate identity for The Founders Bank, a wholly owned subsidiary of Founders Financial Corporation. Designers, Jilly Simons, Steven Canine. ▶

The
FOUNDERS
Bank

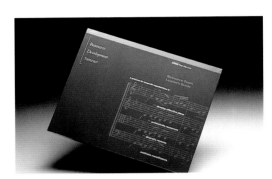

The *Resource Development System* for Peat Marwick Main & Co. includes graphics for a complete boxed set containing facilitator's handbook, manuals, and auditing materials. "We imagined the facilitator as a conductor, the manuals a score, and the four constituencies a quartet." Designers, Jilly Simons, Joe VanDerBos. ▲

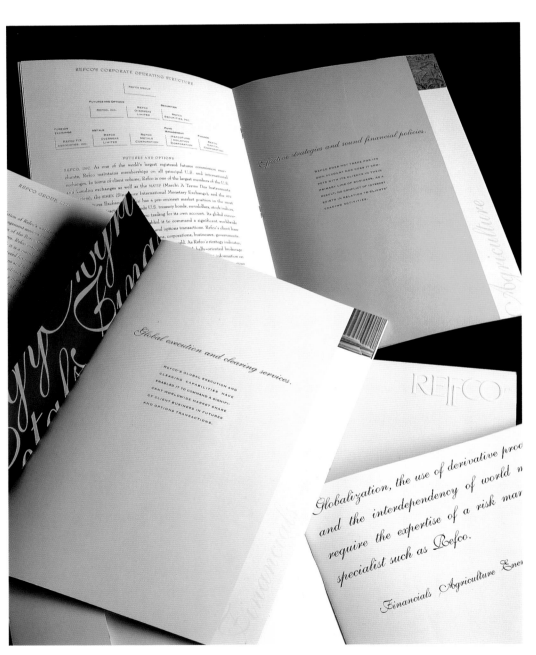

"Things Are Going to Get Ugly" imported paper promotion for Mohawk Paper Mills. Ironic interplay of familiar industrial landscapes, "ugly" text, "homely" photograms, and printing technique demonstrates the beauty and practicality of the papers.

Designers, Jilly Simons, Cindy Chang; Copywriter, Deborah Barron; Photograms, Jilly Simons, David Robson; Photographer, François Robert. ▼

An Entrepreneur's Guide to Going Public, brochure design for Arthur Andersen in which an element of humor was injected by developing provocative illustrative definitions of key terms, i.e., stopwatch, red herring, green shoe. Designers, Jilly Simons, Joe VanDerBos; Photographer, Gordon Meyer. ◄

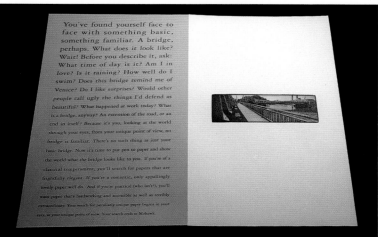 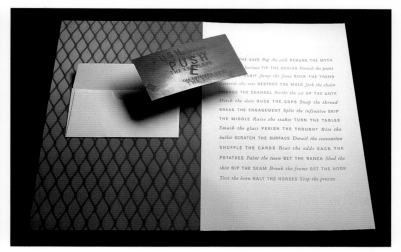

Parent mark identity for The Founders Bank, Founders Financial Corporation was taken from an Ionic column, connoting strength, and a Nautilus shell, giving reference to its location in Florida. Designers, Jilly Simons, David Robson. ◄

"Yo-Yo" and "Bare Bones" advertisements for photographer Christopher Hawker. "Yo-Yo" was commissioned by Atlantic Records for their rap artist by the same name, which gave the inspiration for a visual pun of the classic yo-yo, "unwrapped." Designer, Jilly Simons.
▼

"Fish Polaroid" promotional brochure for photographer Christopher Hawker, known for his unique Polaroid prints. Designers, Jilly Simons, Cindy Chang; Calligrapher, Jilly Simons.
▼

"I Like to Work Hard" graphic icon for photographer Christopher Hawker. Designers, Jilly Simons, David Robson.
◄

No Surprises, Patron's Night promotional piece for Ace Lithographers. The client is a printer and patron of the American Center for Design (ACD). Designers, Jilly Simons, David Robson; Copywriter, Deborah Barron.
▼

Concrete

Identity for a catering and event planning company. The client wanted a mark that echoed their philosophy; contemporary interpretations of classical themes. Designers, Jilly Simons, David Robson.
▶

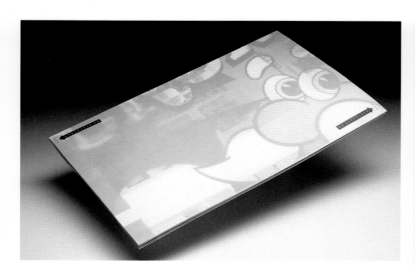

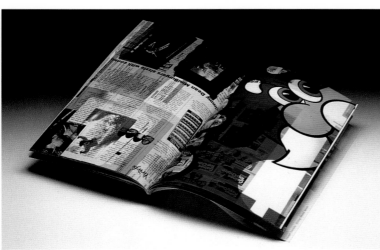

Just Add Color, coloring book for Homeward Bound was developed as a *pro bono* publishing project to benefit the mentally handicapped. It included 36 images donated by such artists as David Salle, Kenny Scharf and Keith Haring. Designers, Jilly Simons, Steven Canine.
▲

32

**Sue Crolick
Advertising and
Design**

Lumber Exchange
Building, Suite 700
10 South Fifth Street
Minneapolis, MN 55402
612/375-9359

Logo design for Sandra
Heinen, artists rep,
Minneapolis, Minnesota.
Designer, Sue Crolick;
Photographer, Mark
LaFavor.

Sue Crolick, Principal
Sue Crolick Advertising
and Design. Photog-
raphy, James Williams.

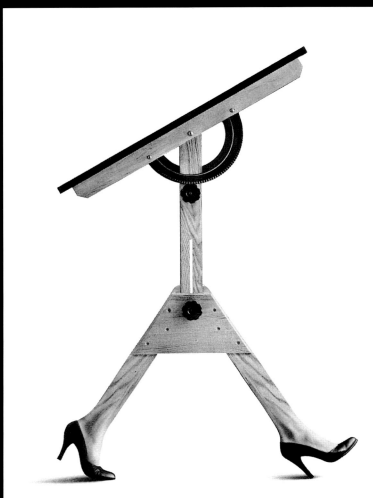

Self-promotional logo
design, Sue T. Crolick
Advertising and Design,
Minneapolis, Minnesota.
Crolick decided the kind
of clients she wanted
were the kind who would
respond to her individ-
uality and humor.
Designer, Sue Crolick.
▼

Principal:
Sue T. Crolick
Year Founded: 1981
Size of Firm: 1
Key Clients:
Architects
Film Companies
Musicians
Typographers
Artist Reps
Voice Talents
Photographers
Copywriters
Ad Agencies
Printers
Theaters
Museums

Sue Crolick Advertising and Design

SUE   T.   CRO   LICK

Now That's A Christmas Tree.

Happy Holidays from Great Faces, the Artists in Advertising Typography.

Give your reader a chuckle, and you give him back something for his time," says Sue Crolick. And for Crolick, humor is a great way to sell. Since opening her own shop in Minneapolis, she has attracted a group of clients consisting, for the most part, of creative people – artist reps, photographers, architects, voice talents, copywriters. She offers them graphic design with the directness and humor often found in advertising. A veteran of top ad agencies, she admits, "I like design that does what advertising does: get an idea across, get an emotional response." Sue's emphasis on personality and a sense of fun in her work is a trademark of her ability to get her clients talents noticed. Sue's awards include Golds from the New York One Show and the New York Art Directors Club, Awards of Excellence from *Communication Arts* magazine, and the annuals of *Graphis*, *Print*, and the American Institute of Graphic Arts, New York. She has also won two Best of Shows from the "Show," Minneapolis. Articles on Sue's work have appeared in *Communication Arts*, *Print*, and *Photodesign*.

Christmas promotion for
Great Faces Typography,
Minneapolis, Minnesota.
Designer, Sue Crolick;
Writer, Kerry Casey;
Typography, Great Faces.
◀

**Sue Crolick
Advertising and
Design**

Direct mail piece for
the Science Museum
of Minnesota, St. Paul,
Minnesota. Copywriter
Tom McElligott assured
Crolick that "There's
NO advertising copy
that can't stand to have a
hole burned through it."
Designer, Sue Crolick;
Writer, Tom McElligott;
Photographers, Kerry
Peterson, Mark LaFavor;
Typography, Great Faces.
▼ ▶

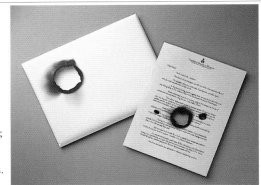

"This is as far as I go," choked the pilot.

"Any closer, we're gonna be marshmallows at a campfire."

Maybe he was right, but I simply had to have the shot.

"Another fifty feet," I replied, the hot sulfur fumes burning my eyes as I squinted through the camera.

"Get me down fifty feet and we'll have it."

Suddenly, the boiling magma below us exploded, twisting us sideways and downward.

Ten yards away a fountain of lava burst into the sky, narrowly missing us as I scrambled to re-focus.

We seemed to be out of control, spinning wildly the fiery maw of certain death.

Next to me, the pilot frantically wrestled through muffled Hail Marys.

"You love it?
You think it's perfect?
It's exactly what you want?
Okay, I'll have him
do it over."

—Joanie Bernstein, worried sick about your satisfaction.
A Jewish mother representing 7 nice young illustrators. (612) 374-3169

Advertisement for
Joanie Bernstein, artists
rep, Minneapolis,
Minnesota. Designer,
Sue Crolick; Copywriter,
Mary Grotting.
◄

Stationery and business
card design for Joan
Ostrin, retail writer,
St. Paul, Minnesota. The
"clothing tag" businesss
card acts as a mark-
down sale notice for
prospective clients.
Designer, Sue Crolick;
Typography, Great
Faces; Photographer,
Mark LaFavor.
▼

Keylines without
the personal touch.

Call Nancy Johnson at 332-1285 for good, clean work.

**Sometimes, you don't find out
you hired the wrong keyliner until it's too late.
until it's too late.**

What good is a new line of type if the old line is still there?
Trust your corrections to a keyliner who does more than paste up type proofs. She *reads* type proofs.
Nancy Johnson, Keyliner 332-1285

**Ifyouaskedfornormalwordspacingandthisiswhatyougot
withnotimetoresetcallNancyJohnsonat332-1285.**

Direct mail promotion
for Nancy Johnson,
keyliner, Minneapolis,
Minnesota. Designer and
Copywriter, Sue Crolick.
▲

36

Sue Crolick Advertising and Design

Christmas card design, Sue Crolick Advertising and Design, Minneapolis, Minnesota; Designer, Sue Crolick; Photographers, Kent Severson, Rod Pierce.
▼ ▶

Photography: Rod Pierce

Logo design for Thacher and Thompson, Architects, Santa Cruz, California. Designer, Sue Crolick; Photographer, Kent Severson.
◀

**Sue Crolick
Advertising and
Design**

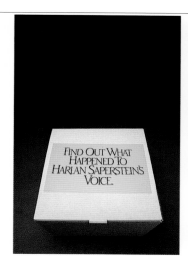

Promotion design for
Harlan Saperstein, voice
talent, Minneapolis,
Minnesota. Harlan
wanted his clients to
know he had a lighter,
funnier sound. A helium
balloon floated up
when the box was
opened. Designer, Sue
Crolick; Typography,
Great Faces; Copywriter,
Joe Alexander.
◄

Stationery designs
for Lake Street Shirts,
Minneapolis, Minnesota.
Designer, Sue Crolick;
Typography, Great
Faces; Mechanical Artist,
Nancy Johnson; Photo-
grapher, Mark LaFavor.
◄

**Sue Crolick
Advertising and
Design**

Direct mail campaign for Kent Severson Photography, Minneapolis, Minnesota. One of a series of ads that focuses on the client's personality as much as his work. Designer and Copywriter, Sue Crolick; Photographer, Kent Severson. ▶

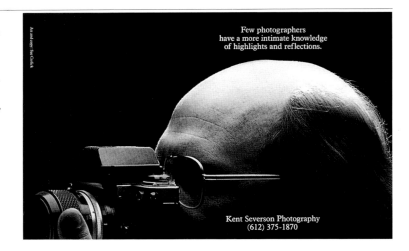

Few photographers
have a more intimate knowledge
of highlights and reflections.

Kent Severson Photography
(612) 375-1870

When it comes to typography, which would you rather have?

The undying gratitude of your company comptroller?

Or one of these?

ONE SHOW AWARD

The next time you come up with a headline you love, call Bill Burk at 1-800-222-6798. We can't guarantee your ledger books will win awards. But there's a good chance your ad will. **Great Faces**
1130 N. Seventh St., Minneapolis, Minnesota 55411

Poster design for Great Faces Typography, Minneapolis, Minnesota. The client's handset type is expensive, but this reminds art directors why it's worth it. Designer, Sue Crolick; Writer, Tom McElligott; Photographer, Kerry Peterson; Typographer, Great Faces Typography. ▲

Logo design for Joe Giannetti Photography, possibly the only Italian photographer in Minneapolis. Designer, Sue Crolick; Photographer, Joe Giannetti. ▶

Direct mail promotion for Richard Hamilton Smith Photography, St. Paul, Minnesota. Designer, Sue Crolick; Writer, Gary LaMaster; Photographer, Richard Hamilton Smith.

►

Direct mail campaign for Kent Severson Photography, Minneapolis, Minnesota. One of a series of ads that focuses on the client's personality as much as his work. Designer and Copywriter, Sue Crolick; Photographer, Kent Severson.

►

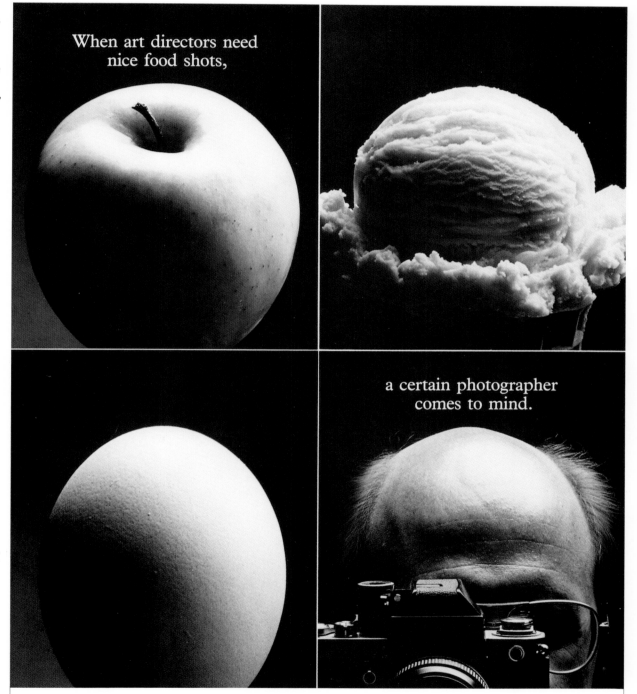

**Drenttel Doyle
Partners**

1123 Broadway
New York, NY 10010
212/463-8787

Left to right:
Pamela Salandy, William
Drenttel, Miguel Oks,
Ann Rickey, Thomas
Kluepfel, Stephen Doyle,
Gary Tooth, John Kubalak,
Mats Hakansson, Danae
Camillos, Rosemarie Turk,
Charles Robertson.
▼

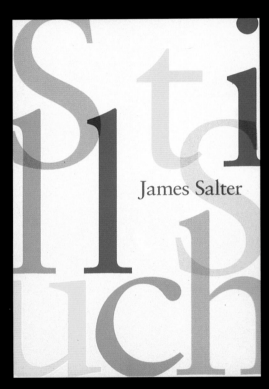

James Salter

Book cover design of
Still Such by James Salter,
private edition published
by William Drenttel,
New York, New York,
1992. Designer, Stephen
Doyle.
▲

Cover designs and logo
application for The
Industry, a magazine
prototype covering media
in all its late 20th-century
forms. New York, New
York, 1992. Creative
Director, Stephen Doyle;
Designer, Andrew Gray.
▼ ▶

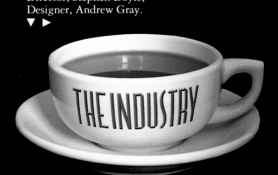

Principals:
William Drenttel
Stephen Doyle
Thomas Kluepfel
Year Founded: 1985
Size of Firm: 12
Clients:
Brooklyn Academy of Music,
Champion International Corporation,
Equitable Real Estate,
Cooper-Hewitt Museum,
Christian Science Monitor/World Monitor Magazine,
Elektra Entertainment,
HarperCollins,

Loews Hotels,
Museum of Modern Art,
National Audubon Society,
New York Zoological Society,
Olympia & York/ The World Financial Center,
Showtime Networks,
Spy Magazine,
Time Warner Magazine Company.

Drenttel Doyle Partners

When it was formed seven years ago, Drenttel Doyle Partners' goal was to merge expertise in graphic design, communications, advertising, and marketing in a small studio environment. Today, with a staff of 12 and a broad roster of clients, DDP has largely succeeded in that goal; it is an office where such diverse projects as advertising, identity programs, brochures and collateral material, magazines, catalogs, books, albums, installations and signage, and products are created simultaneously. Behind this varied output of creative energy is a central idea that each project is approached as a unique challenge—from display piece to timepiece—whether it calls for refined elegance, hard-hitting directness, a little humor or all of these. In uniting the various disciplines of editorial design, corporate communications, multi-dimensional graphics and advertising, DDP serves the interests of the individual client while producing work that remains sharply personal.

Drenttel Doyle Time Tables line of watches, feature "Rush Hours," "Oven Timer," "Rotary Dial," "Shutter Speed," and "Fuel Gauge" designs. Designer, Thomas Kluepfel; Project Manager, William Drenttel. ▲

Spy Magazine fashion supplement poses the question: "If Thomas Jefferson were alive today, what would he wear?" (Would you believe Matsuda?) Creative Director, Stephen Doyle; Designer, Rosemarie Turk; Photographer, Joseph Astor. ▶

Drenttel Doyle Partners

Site specific banner installation, 1991, for the World Financial Center/Olympia & York. Designer, Stephen Doyle; Project Manager, William Drenttel; Architects, FTL Associates.
▼

Half-title and lead essay from Dislocations exhibition catalog, for The Musuem of Modern Art, New York, New York, 1991. Exploring the exhibition's theme of dislocation, DDP disarranged the usual sequence of pages in the catalog, as well as incorporating typographic hijinks. Creative Director, Stephen Doyle; Designer, Andrew Gray; Project Manager, William Drenttel; Photographer, Scott Frances; MoMA Design Manager, Michael Hentges.
▶

Program poster, for the holiday season at the World Financial Center, for Olympia & York. Designer, Stephen Doyle; Illustrator, Etienne Delessert.
▶

Holiday product catalog, 1991, featuring upscale retailers at the World Financial Center, for Olympia & York. Designer, Rosemarie Turk; Photographer, Darryl Patterson; Copywriter, Gail Friedman.
▶

**Drenttel Doyle
Partners**

Kiosk, text panel, fence signage, and title from "A Design Resource" exhibition at the Cooper-Hewitt Museum, New York, New York, 1991. Utilizing huge books, the installation conveys the concept of a "visual library" in a dramatic manner, carrying the graphic identity out into the street. Designers, Stephen Doyle, Andrew Gray; Project Manager, William Drenttel.
▼

"Flix" movie cable channel logo, 1992, for Showtime Networks. Designer, Mats Hakansson. ◄

Natalie Cole "Unforgettable" album cover, for Elektra Entertainment, New York, New York, 1991. Legendary Hollywood photographer George Hurrell shot Cole in an image that repositioned her pop status and evoked the era of her father's classic songs. Designer, Stephen Doyle; Photographer, George Hurrell. ▼

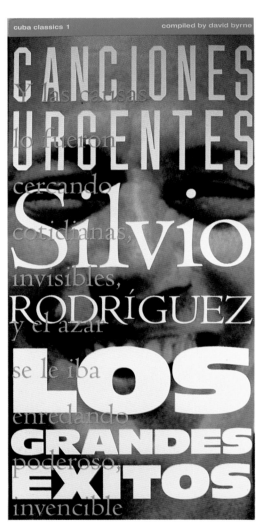

Silvio Rodriguez "Los Grandes Exitos" CD package, from David Byrne's World Classics series, for Luaka Bop/Warner Bros., New York, New York. Designers, Stephen Doyle, Andrew Gray; Photographer, Yale Evelev. ▲

Idjah Hadidjah "Tonggeret" album cover for Icon/Elektra Nonesuch, New York, New York. The album is a collection of music in the Jaipong style from Sunda, Indonesia. Designer, Stephen Doyle. ◄

Barneys New York Windows, 1991, three from a series of ten window displays commissioned from ten illustrators to celebrate the 10th anniversary of American Illustration, New York, New York. Creative Director, Stephen Doyle; Windows by, top to bottom, Stephen Doyle, Henrick Drescher, Anita Kunz.
▼

Drenttel Doyle Partners

Spread and cover design of Courtland Gloss paper promotion, 1992, for Champion International Corporation, Stamford, Connecticut. Designer, Stephen Doyle; Photographer, Brian Hill; Copywriter, Danny Altman.
▼

"Straight Talk" advertising campaign series, 1991, for Champion International Corporation, Stamford, Connecticut. The ads, which ran in Time and the Wall Street Journal, address the issue of recycling. Creative Director and Copywriter, Thomas Kluepfel; Designer, Andrew Gray.
▼

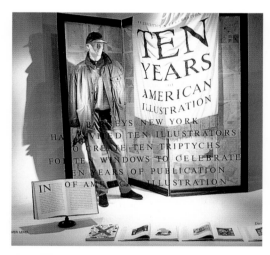

Hand-painted portfolio box and brochure promotion launch of Martha Stewart's Living Magazine, 1991, for Time Warner Magazine Company, New York, New York. Designers, Stephen Doyle, Rosemarie Turk. ▼

Cover design of Roget's Thesaurus, 1992, for HarperCollins Publishers, New York, New York. Designer, Stephen Doyle. ▶

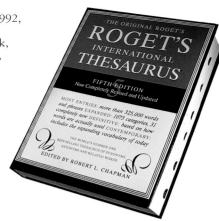

I usually can't make up my mind what to wear. It takes me hours to get out of my own house. Therefore I never get around to thinking what's in other people's houses. It's Greek to me whether I'm going to sit on a rose-red or royal-blue damask chair. Maybe I'm deficient that way.— Then, I had to read about Pauline's death. She told her friends that she wanted to pass away in her best court dress. That was the only way, she said, to meet His Majesty Death.—I tried to get myself to laugh. I would meet His Majesty naked, I told myself. But now the idea of dying became very

Text and fashion spreads from the Kathleen Madden fashion catalog, 1991, for Gottfried Helnwein/Kathleen Madden, New York, New York. Designer, Stephen Doyle; Photographer, Gottfried Helnwein; Author, Norman Mailer. ▲

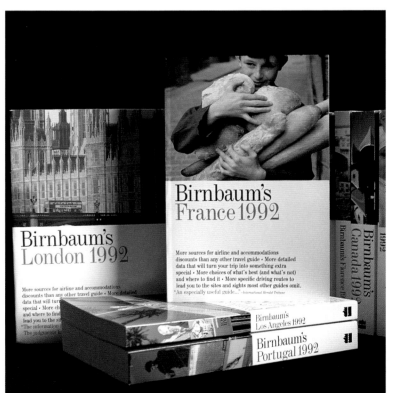

Birnbaum's Travel Guides cover designs, 1991-92, for HarperCollins Publishers, New York, New York. The series will eventually encompass over 100 titles, updated annually. Creative Director, Stephen Doyle; Designer, Andrew Gray; Photographers, Various. ◀

Cover designs of series of college outline texts, for HarperCollins Publishers, 1991-92. The objective was to breathe new life into the staid study guide section of the bookstores. Creative Director, Stephen Doyle; Designers, Agnethe Glatved, Christopher Johnson; Photographers and Illustrators, Various.
▼

Drenttel Doyle Partners

Covers format for World Monitor Magazine redesign, 1991. Creative Director, Stephen Doyle; Designer, Rosemarie Turk; World Monitor Art Director, Laura Frank; Photographers, Various.
▼

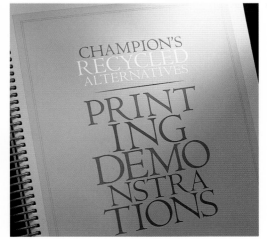

"Recycled Alternatives" swatch book, 1991, for Champion International Corporation, Stamford, Connecticut. Creative Director, Thomas Kluepfel; Designers, Thomas Kluepfel, Agnethe Glatved.
◄

Logo design and
stationery system for
Ema Design, Denver,
Colorado. Ema's identity
expresses his passion
for simplicity. Art
Director and Designer,
Thomas Ema.
▼

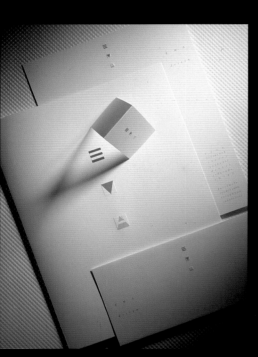

Ema Design's moving
and open house
announcements feature
Denver's historic
Larimer Square, the
site of the new offices.
Art Director and
Designer, Thomas Ema.
▶

Ema Design

Poster for the Design Center at the Ice House, Denver, Colorado. The geometry of the nautilus is the graphic anchor for this poster announcing a major architectural and interior design conference. Art Director and Designer, Thomas Ema.

▼

Principal:
Thomas C. Ema
Year Founded: 1982
Size of Firm: 2
Key Clients:
Adolph Coors Company,
Aren Design,
Art Directors' Club
of Denver,
CLGS Incorporated,
Design Center at
the Ice House,
Gerrity Oil & Gas
Corporation,
Gritz-Ritter Graphics,
Kresin-Wingard,
McDATA Corporation,
Mental Health
Association of Colorado,
Neenah Paper Company,
Plains Petroleum
Company,
Swedish Medical Center

DESIGN EXCHANGE 8 8

FUTURES

29.30
April
1 9 8 8

THE DESIGN CENTER
AT THE ICE HOUSE
DENVER 298.9191

Thomas Ema develops design solutions that reflect his philosophy of balanced contrasts: "You have to listen to your client's needs with one ear. With the other ear, you have to listen to your own heart." Yet Ema's design style—rich with understated passion—is far from traditional. Look closely and you will see visual statements that strike a graceful balance between extremes: soothing textural patterns sheathed by hard-edged structural elements; large, bold type softened by italics; gloss and dull varnishes that transform two dimensions into three. "Having grown up in Williamsburg, Virginia, I have a deep appreciation for history and enduring quality," states Ema. Perhaps this explains why his work is imbued with a sense of timelessness that transcends trends and fads. Ema's childhood ardor for painting watercolor landscapes of the Blue Ridge Mountains found its sharp focus at the Kansas City Art Institute, where he studied Bauhaus design. He has said that he knew his schooling was complete when he "learned to paint with type."

Annual report for Adolph Coors Company, Golden, Colorado. Developed within the context of the company's existing design guidelines, the report heightens the Coors public image. Art Director and Designer, Thomas Ema.
▼

Corporate brochure for Swedish Medical Center, Englewood, Colorado. The hospital's philosophy of care and its flagship programs are clearly represented to its key audiences. Designers, Thomas Ema and Debra Johnson-Humphrey.
▼

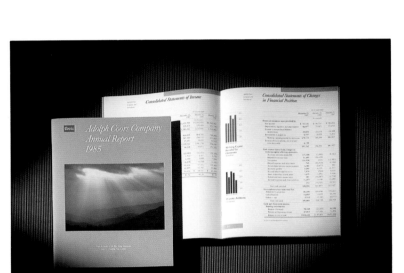

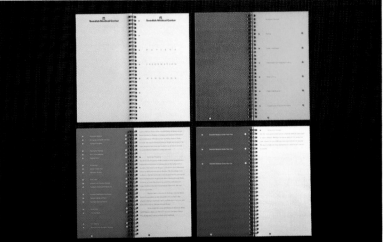

Annual report for McDATA Corporation, Broomfield, Colorado. In addition to providing financial data, this annual report made highly technical information accessible through design. Designers, Thomas Ema and Debra Johnson-Humphrey.
▲

Design of the Swedish Medical Center Patient Information Handbook fills a functional need with a creative solution. Designers, Thomas Ema and Debra Johnson-Humphrey.
▲

Annual and quarterly reports for Plains Petroleum Company, Lakewood, Colorado feature stunning landscape imagery for a unique identity. Art Director and Designer, Thomas Ema.
▼

Identity and annual report for Gerrity Oil & Gas Corporation, Denver, Colorado uses strong blue and black graphic elements to symbolize the company's primary products. Designers, Thomas Ema and Debra Johnson-Humphrey.
◄

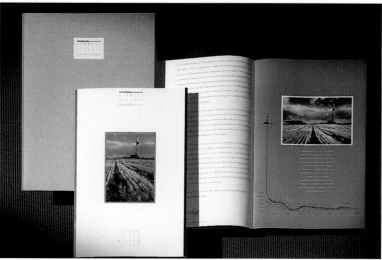

The Best of Corporate
Art in America,
catalog designs for
1999 Broadway,
Denver, Colorado. Art
Director and Designer,
Thomas Ema.
▼

Brochure for Aren
Design, Vail, Colorado.
The company is a wood
and metalworking
firm that crafts exquisite
custom products for
architectural applications.
Art Director and
Designer, Thomas Ema.
▼

Logo, stationery package and brochure for Kresin-Wingard, Chicago, Illinois. The logo for this recruitment firm served as "building blocks" for the brochure design. Art Director and Designer, Thomas Ema.

▼

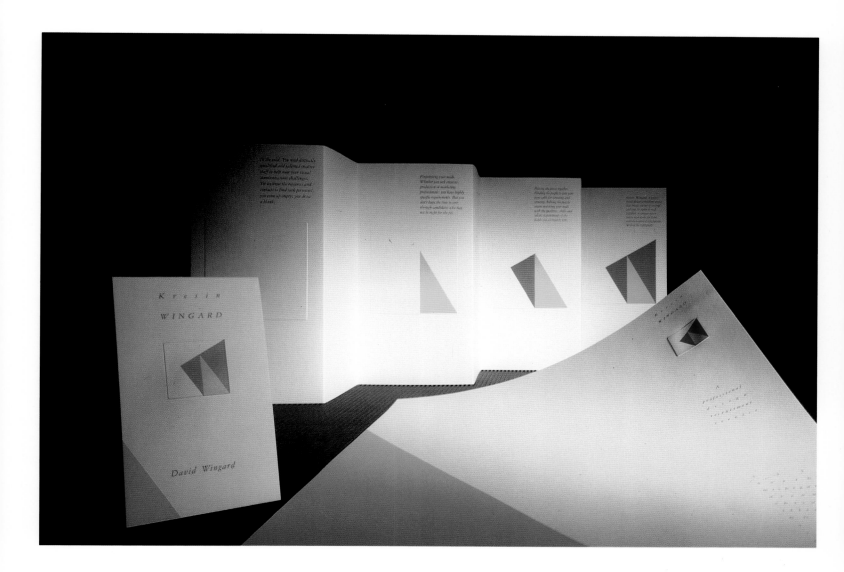

James Cross announce-
ment for the Art
Directors' Club, of
Denver. Cross's name
and reputation provided
an irreverent concept of
"reverence." Art
Director and Designer,
Thomas Ema.
▼

To announce Pentagram's
Peter Harrison's arrival,
"the British are coming"
served to encourage
member attendence
at the Art Directors' Club
of Denver. Art Director
and Designer, Thomas
Ema.
▼

Fritz Gottschalk poster
for Art Directors' Club
of Denver, Colorado.
International passport
stamps are used as
design elements for this
poster announcing
Gottschalk's lecture—
on his design of the new
Swiss passport. Art
Director and Designer,
Thomas Ema.
▲

Program announcing
Michael Bierut lecture at
the Art Directors' Club
of Denver borrows a
number of signature
Vignelli design elements
and a strong dash of
humor. Art Director and
Designer, Thomas Ema.
▶

Ema Design

Corporate identity and stationery system for CLGS Incorporated, Denver, Colorado. The company name was whimsically related to the fact that the president of this executive "head-hunting" firm always wears clogs. The business card features "postion-to-be-filled" holes. Designers, Thomas Ema and Debra Johnson-Humphrey. ▼

Letterhead sample folder for Kimberly Writing line of paper for Neenah Paper Company. Designers, Thomas Ema and Debra Johnson-Humphrey. ▼

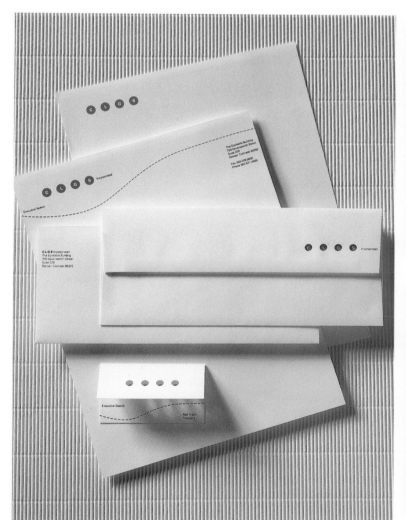

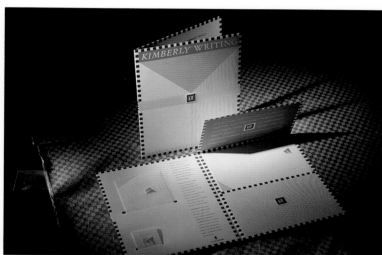

Logo, stationery package and T-shirt for the Mile High Friendship Walk sponsored by Mental Health Association of Colorado. Designers, Thomas Ema and Debra Johnson-Humphrey. ◀

Desk calendar design for Gritz-Ritter Graphics, Colorado is a statement of environmental concern for the life forms in the sea. Designers, Thomas Ema and Debra Johnson-Humphrey. ▲

Bill Drenttel spent nine years in advertising – traveling extensively on business and collecting books in his spare time to stay sane. In 1986 he co-founded Drenttel Doyle Partners to find a way to merge design and marketing in a studio environment. The firm expanded in 1992 to include Drenttel Doyle Projects, focused on three-dimensional design projects. Bill spends his free time collecting books, and under the imprint William Drenttel New York, publishes literary works by such writers as Paul Auster and James Salter. He is on the boards of the Poetry Society of America and the AIGA.

New York Views

William Drenttel

From the vantage of the streets, New York is still a bustling, decaying metropolis. The homeless that walk the streets know that they came before the Crash, before the other hordes of people now out of work. Twenty stories up, though, the nighttime skyline is cheerful, the city having discovered that skyscrapers can be lit the color of cotton candy.

For the past ten years, I have lived ten stories above the beginning of Madison Avenue. Halfway between the street and the skyline, the view is stunning yet full of contrasts. My sense of the city has been shaped here: it's one place where the city is quiet, in the distance. Nevertheless, the contrasts seem to accumulate, like a residue of the last awkward decade.

When I came to New York in the mid-70's, the Frick and Morgan mansions held a certain stature for newcomers; they housed great private collections, presented in homes whose architectural reference was to urban homes in other cities. The mansion popular today is Ralph Lauren's; it anchors a barren Madison Avenue, housing a store whose retail success stems from reference to the opulence of country homes. This is a strange contrast, I think.

Opera once represented New York at its most elitist. Now it's sung to subtitles at Lincoln Center, performed outdoors in Central Park and sells out the Brooklyn Academy of Music, home of the avant-garde New Wave Festival. (To enjoy classic opera in the home of Robert Wilson and Laurie Anderson is another contrast, this one a twist on the populist spirit.)

Thanks to the late Joe Papp and the Public Theater, there is plenty of Shakespeare performed today, but there's little work for the best classical actors—Hollywood stars like to do "Shakespeare in the Park" on their vacations.

Broadway, having died so many times, set new revenue records this year as musical revivals swept the Tonys. High-priced pseudo-theater booms and the Times Square Redevelopment Plans wilt in the recession.

The art market, too, died abruptly a couple of years ago. Yet the Guggenheim, the Morgan Library, the Brooklyn Museum and the Jewish Museum have recently expanded. Last summer, a second Guggenheim opened five miles south in SoHo (showing "modern" in the heartland of "contemporary"), and franchised outposts in Spain and Austria are on the horizon. The Museum of Modern Art, under pressure to be more *contemporary*, did a major exhibition of installation art in 1992. Business goes on. The Whitney, on the other hand, can't get its new building built, putting this institution in a holding pattern. A dead art market expanding—and more contrasts.

In the heyday after *Spy* magazine, every magazine in America seemed the object of a redesign. Advertising dies. The magazine world weakens. *Time* magazine is redesigned. In the same year, "all the news that's fit to print" looks different—*The New York Times*, too, has been redesigned. (Also, the former *Spy* editor moved to *Vanity Fair*, and the *Vanity Fair* editor moved to *The New Yorker*.) Like the movie industry in Los Angeles, we take a certain pride in the chaos of our local industries: the media is *ours* after all.

The demise of Scribners on Fifth Avenue did not mean the end of great bookstores in New York. Between Books & Co. and the Strand one can still find books. The larger publishing industry also continues to fuel the city—with energy as much as money—despite its own wave of mergers and a myopic focus on bestsellers.

Music is a category that's perhaps richer in 1992 than before the Crash (the same year CD's began to replace albums in records shops; only a year later they passed albums in sales). World music, new music, even popular music finds musicians traveling the globe and merging what they hear elsewhere into their own music. Encouragingly, music is one industry where being pluralistic and multicultural seems to come naturally.

In film, there's a phenomenon of mass not variety. Cineplex Odeon has brought 22 cinemas and 154 screens to Manhattan and there are now theaters in every neighborhood, even the East Village. There are, however, fewer movies to see, and the revival film houses have been subsumed or disappeared.

In fashion, style is now often achieved through scale. Nike owns Times Square. DKNY takes over Herald Square. The Gap controls bus stops. This industry's sad sidebar are the obituaries every day of fashion people dead from AIDS.

New York was not taken over by Benneton. Bendel's faded, sold and then expanded under the sponsorship of The Limited, another player. Bonwit Teller, B. Altman's and Alexander's are gone. The Gaps everywhere are clean and bright. Macy's hangs in there by a Wall Street thread. Bergdorf's goes catecorner after the men's market. Bloomingdale's sold, expanded, almost died, and now survives. Barneys New York is expanding uptown, and with Japanese money, to Chicago and Los Angeles; having grown up in New York, they at least carry on the venerable department store tradition of livening the street with great store windows.

Higher up, the skyline itself has been fundamentally transformed. What began with the Citibank Tower in the mid-70's perhaps ended when the Colosseum project at Columbus Circle stalled in 1989. In between came the "9" at 9 West 57th Street, the AT&T and IBM towers, atriums, sliver buildings, Battery Park City, art pockets and pocket parks, and, of course, Donald Trump. A pause and then more building: Memphis and Red Square, IDCNY, that circus-pink thing on Herald Square, and The World Financial Center. So much tax-abated building, and only a few examples of distinction.

In observing change, noting its occurence, one almost inherently sounds nostalgic. But, like other cities, New York City does *look* different and the cultural climate *is* different. The expansions and contradictions that were exciting are now often painful. From most perspectives the result has not been stagnation, but its opposite—a bizarre kind of momentum in a narrower landscape.

In this confusing context, we do business. There's still immense commerce out there, and more designers and more work. Design is thriving. Like the city, though, the design profession has it own contrasts. Pentagram added three partners last year. Last August, "The Today Show" featured designers doing fake campaigns to package the presidential candidates; anything and everything can be redesigned in 1992. We're news. Meanwhile, John Burgee and Philip Johnson are bankrupt and another 2,000 architects have lost their jobs in the past two years. The truth is, out on the streets, many graphic designers are hurting too.

Most of the firms in this book were founded and prospered in the 1980's when business was booming. In New York, however, most of us did not make our reputations on the coattails of Wall Street. But we participated in, even made money from, work that has changed the landscape around us.

The question, even in one's own city, is how one finds a critical view on such changes, and thereby on one's own work. The Crash, after all, changed little but continues to be a point of reference for almost everything. Maybe we need a new point of reference—one that looks critically, accepts complexity, and acknowledges that there are in fact other more fundamental social changes that have occurred. Finding quality in what's out there and creating it in what we build is not a question of recession or growth. It will not happen simply because we recycle. Less-is-more and no-frills maxims don't help much either. We even may be able to live with one less department store; maybe with fewer magazines, movie theaters and museums. But we cannot thrive by denying the complexity around us. And we cannot live well, long-term, with a rampant and blind reconfiguration—and in the process, redesign—of every aspect of our lives. This, I fear, is why the view seems so daunting.

**Peter Good
Graphic Design**

3 North Main Street
Chester, CT 06412
203/526-9597

Janet Cummings Good,
Peter Good, Susan
Fasick-Jones, from left
to right. Photographer,
Sean Kernan.
▼

Illustration for
Strathmore Paper
swatch book using the
thistle mark in sewn
fabric. Illustrator, Peter
Good; Art Director,
Mike Scricco.
▼

Identity for Strathmore
Paper Company,
Westfield, Massachusetts.
The mark is a simplified
thistle that adapts to
various sizes and repro-
duction techniques. Art
Director, Mike Scricco.
◄

Principals:
Peter Good,
Susan Fasick-Jones,
Janet Cummings Good.
Year Founded: 1971
Size of Firm: 8
Key Clients:
Aetna,
Arjo-Wiggins,
Champion International,
The Hartford Steam
Boiler Inspection
and Insurance Co.,
Merck & Co., Inc.,
Mystic Seaport Museum,
National Theatre
of the Deaf,

Northeast Magazine,
Strathmore Paper
Company,
TheaterWorks,
The United States
Postal Service,
United Technologies,
The Wadsworth
Atheneum

Peter Good Graphic Design

Peter Good Graphic Design believes that a simple truth of communication is that its effectiveness changes as perceptions of words and images change. They understand that it is not a matter of adhering to learned doctrine, but an organic process, always evolving in response to complex and dynamic needs. The inspiration for their design solutions comes from the richness of the external world. The encouragement of a nurturing and collaborative open relationship within the office also extends to every client. The firm seeks challenges in that elusive combination of the unexpected and unfamiliar, yet appropriate and accessible. Their goal: to compel someone to stop, think, react and remember.

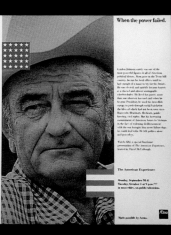

The American Experience is an annual comprehensive design project for public television.

Poster announcement of the series The American Experience, for Aetna, Hartford, Connecticut. Designers, Peter Good, Janet Cummings Good, Susan Fasick-Jones; Copywriter, Gordon Bowman.
▲

Promotion materials, The American Experience. Designers, Peter Good, Ed Kim, Susan Fasick-Jones, Paula Lawyer; Copywriter, Gordon Bowman; Illustrators, Peter Good, Janet Cummings Good.
▲

Advertising, The American Experience. Designer, Susan Fasick-Jones; Copywriter, Gordon Bowman.
▶

Wadsworth Atheneum: Of the World, slipcase and brochure designs for the Wadsworth Atheneum, Hartford, Connecticut. Designers, Peter Good, Susan Fasick-Jones; Copywriter, Fritz Jellinghaus; Photographer, Robert Lisak.
▼

**Peter Good
Graphic Design**

Atheneum, newsletter for the Wadsworth Atheneum, Hartford, Connecticut. Designer, Peter Good; Copywriter, Guthrie Sayen.
▼

Button, "At the Wadsworth Atheneum, Art speaks all languages," for the Wadsworth Atheneum, Hartford, Connecticut. Designer and Illustrator, Peter Good.
▶

At the Wadsworth Atheneum
Art speaks all languages

En el Wadsworth Atheneum, el arte habla todos los idiomas

Visite el Wadsworth Atheneum en el 600 de la Calle Main, en Hartford, Connecticut.
Gracias a United Technologies por este mensaje

Spanish language bus shelter poster for the Wadsworth Atheneum/United Technologies, Hartford, Connecticut. Designer, Peter Good.
▲

September   October   November   1989

Atheneum

A   U   T   U   M   N

Robin Winters, as artist in residence, will install one gallery with inspirational objects and another with works inspired by those objects. The result: an object lesson in how the creative mind operates. See page 4.

Robert Mapplethorpe's photographs seize the eye and stop the heart. They are classically beautiful, stunningly original and very disturbing — so disturbing that one museum backed out of its plans to show them. See page 5.

The entire second floor of the Morgan Building has been renovated and rearranged to display more masterpieces. The centerpiece of the new installation evokes a treasure room in a Baroque palace. See page 6.

Barbara Hudson is about to set two records at the Wadsworth Atheneum. She will be the museum's first African-American curator and the museum's first curator of African-American art. See page 6.

Two exhibitions commemorating the centennial of Vincent Van Gogh's death will bring together the largest collection of his paintings and drawings ever assembled. A group will go to the Netherlands to see them. See Page 6.

Is some art so offensive it ceases to be art? A panel of critics and art historians will discuss this question — so relevant to this fall's major exhibitions. The panel will then field questions from the audience. See page 8.

This fall is the season of outrage. The first major exhibition comprises Dada and Surrealist works once considered offensive in the extreme. Most of the fall programs – films, lectures, a concert, a workshop – are designed to complement the show. The second major exhibition is a retrospective of the late Robert Mapplethorpe. Like the Dadaists and Surrealists in their time, Mapplethorpe is provoking extreme reactions in his. ⊠

Ceci n'est pas une pipe.

The inscription above reads, "This is not a pipe." The painter, Rene Magritte, is making a point that is central to this fall's major exhibition, *The Dada and Surrealist Word-Image*, sponsored by Bronson & Hutensky. Magritte painted *The Treachery of Images* in 1928-29. It is now owned by the Los Angeles County Museum of Art. For more information on the show and this painting, see page 3. ⟫⟫⟫→

150th anniversary poster for the Wadsworth Atheneum, Hartford, Connecticut, combines the architecture of the museum with art from the collection. Designer, Peter Good.
▼

Annual report front and back cover for the Wadsworth Atheneum, Hartford, Connecticut. Designers, Susan Fasick-Jones, Peter Good; Photographer, Joseph Szaszfai.
▶

Summer Music at Harkness Park 1990, poster for Summer Music, Incorporated, New London, Connecticut. Designer and Illustrator, Peter Good.
▼

Moondance, DaDa, Piazza Del Sole invitations, tickets and envelope for the Wadsworth Atheneum, Hartford, Connecticut. Designer and Illustrator, Peter Good.
◀

**Peter Good
Graphic Design**

The Enveloping Herbs is a promotional package for converters who use Champion paper for envelopes. For Champion International, Stamford, Connecticut. Designer, Peter Good; Illustrators, Janet Cummings Good, Peter Good; Writer, Thomas Mann. ▼

Symbol for the Hartford Whalers National Hockey League team, Hartford, Connecticut. Designer, Peter Good. ▶

One Hundred and Twenty-Five: Full Steam Ahead, 125th anniversary poster for The Hartford Steam Boiler Inspection and Insurance Company, Hartford, Connecticut. The locomotive is based on the corporate symbol. Designer and Illustrator, Peter Good. ▼

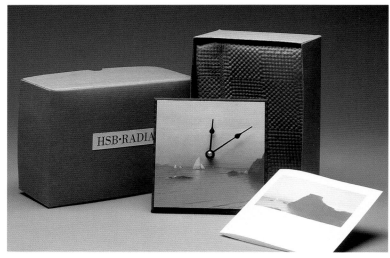

Hartford Steam Boiler Inspection And Insurance Company Turns One Hundred And Twenty-Five Full Steam Ahead!

Desk clock for H.S.B Radian, Hartford, Connecticut, commemorates an environmental seminar. The image on the clock face is a reproduction from the corporation's fine art collection. Designers, Peter Good, Susan Fasick-Jones; Fabricator, Portfoliobox. ▲

Identity and packaging design for Nathan Hale Golden Lager, Hartford, Connecticut. Designers, Peter Good, Janet Cummings Good. ▶

Manchester String Quartet, poster design for Merck & Co., Inc., Rahway, New Jersey. Designer and Illustrator, Peter Good.
▼

**Peter Good
Graphic Design**

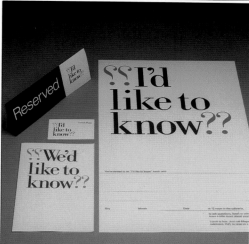

"I'd Like to Know," for Champion International, Stamford, Connecticut. The program seeks to enhance communication between management and employees by means of informal question-and-answer lunches. Designer, Peter Good.
◄

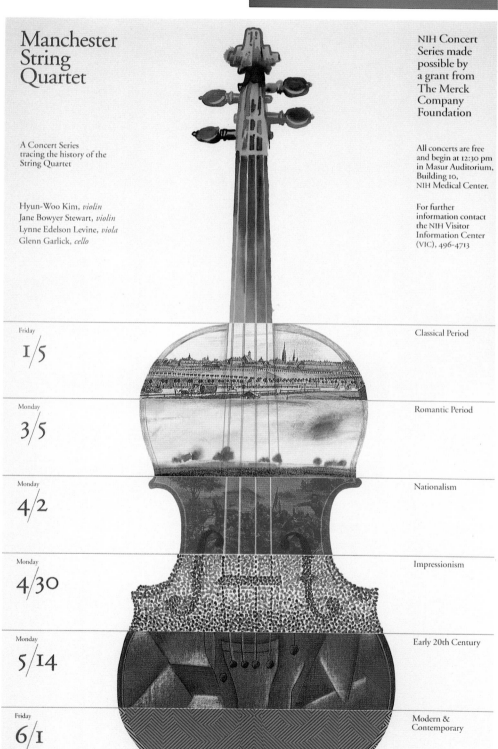

Manchester
String
Quartet

A Concert Series
tracing the history of the
String Quartet

Hyun-Woo Kim, *violin*
Jane Bowyer Stewart, *violin*
Lynne Edelson Levine, *viola*
Glenn Garlick, *cello*

NIH Concert
Series made
possible by
a grant from
The Merck
Company
Foundation

All concerts are free
and begin at 12:30 pm
in Masur Auditorium,
Building 10,
NIH Medical Center.

For further
information contact
the NIH Visitor
Information Center
(VIC), 496-4713

Friday
1/5
Classical Period

Monday
3/5
Romantic Period

Monday
4/2
Nationalism

Monday
4/30
Impressionism

Monday
5/14
Early 20th Century

Friday
6/1
Modern &
Contemporary

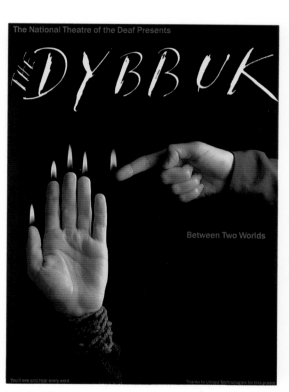

The Dybbuk, poster design for the National Theatre of the Deaf, Chester, Connecticut. Designer, Peter Good; Photographer, Sally Andersen-Bruce.
▲

Our Children at Risk,
poster design for Merck
& Co., Inc., Rahway,
New Jersey. Designer,
Peter Good; Photog-
rapher, Melanie Barocas.
▼

Artifact, circa 1850,
poster design for
Mystic Seaport Museum,
Mystic, Connecticut.
Designer, Susan Fasick-
Jones; Photographer,
Mary Ann Stets;
Illustrator (border),
Timothy Eastland.
◄

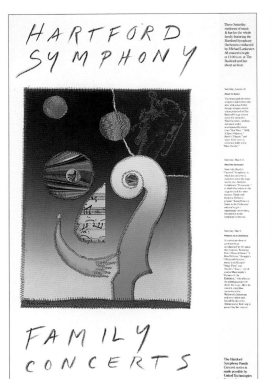

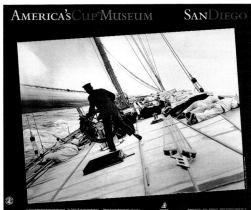

Hartford Symphony
Family Concerts, poster
design for United
Technologies, Hartford,
Connecticut. Designer
and Illustrator, Peter
Good.
▲

A Child, poster design
commemorating the
International Year of
the Child, for Philips
Medical Systems,
Incorporated, Shelton,
Connecticut. Designer,
Peter Good; Photo-
grapher, John Van
Schalkwyk; Writer,
Sharon Herlihy.
▶

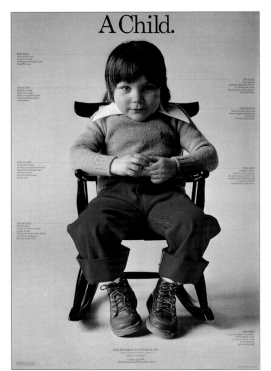

Video box, brochure
and inside spread of The
Campaign for Mystic
Seaport, for Mystic
Seaport Museum, Mystic,
Connecticut. Designers,
Susan Fasick-Jones,
Peter Good, Janet
Cummings Good.
▲

America's Cup Museum
of San Diego, poster
design for Mystic Seaport
Museum, Mystic,
Connecticut. Designer,
Susan Fasick-Jones;
Photography, Rosenfeld
Collection.
▲

**Peter Good
Graphic Design**

TheaterWorks '86-'87, first of a series of posters for TheaterWorks, Hartford, Connecticut. Designer and Illustrator, Peter Good; Photography, Garrison and Coon.
▼

Annual report cover design for Society for Savings Bancorp, Inc., Hartford, Connecticut. Designers, Peter Good, Susan Fasick-Jones; Photographer, Jim Coon.
◀

TheaterWorks '91-'92, poster design for TheaterWorks, Hartford, Connecticut. Designer and Illustrator, Peter Good; Photographer, Jim Coon.
▲

Graphic Design
2970 Olcott Road
Big Flats, NY 14814
607/562-8681

Left to right:
Peter C.G. Harp,
MacGregor D. Harp,
Linda E. Wagner,
Susan C. Harp and
Douglas G. Harp of
Harp and Company.
▼

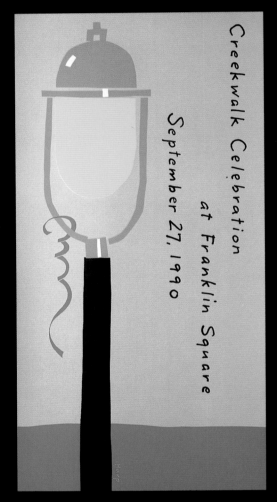

Creekwalk Celebration
at Franklin Square
September 27, 1990

Poster commemorat-
ing the renovation
and revitalization of
Creekwalk, an area
of downtown Syracuse,
for Eric Mower &
Associates, Syracuse,
New York. Designer,
Douglas G. Harp.
▲

"oz ne" T-shirt, origin-
ally designed for
ADPSR 1990 Social
Issues Postcard
Competition, New
York, New York.
Designer, Douglas
G. Harp.
◄

Harp and Company

Principals:
Douglas G. Harp,
Susan C. Harp
Year Founded: 1989
Size of Firm: 3
Key Clients:
ADPSR,
The Bibb Company,
Children's Museum
of Manhattan,
Children's Hospital
at Dartmouth,
Herbert F. Johnson
Museum of Art at
Cornell University,
Corning Incorporated,
Corning Museum
of Glass,
Dartmouth-Hitchcock
Medical Center,
Fisher Hotels Group,
Green Alternatives,
Hangar Theatre,
Mohawk Paper Mills,
Rochester Tel,
Smithsonian Institution
Traveling Exhibition
Service,
The Spence School,
The NTC Group,
Valley Montessori
School

Promotional poster
for Valley Montessori
School, Big Flats, New
York. The watercolor
was painted by the
designer's two-and-a-
half-year-old son and
used when this project
came along. Illustrator,
MacGregor D. Harp;
Copywriter, Douglas G.
Harp.
▲

Logo design and appli-
cation, AIDS Awareness
Day/A Day Without
Art, for the Institute
for Human Services,
Corning, New York.
Designers, Susan C.
Harp, Douglas G. Harp.
▶

Harp and Company, founded in 1989, has an uncomplicated approach to design: The solution must communicate the client's message simply and clearly, using interesting and thoughtful typography. An unexpected twist and a dash of wit are then added to complete their recipe for good design. They are a young firm, which means fresh ideas, but Harp and Company is grounded in experience, which ensures skill in applying those ideas to a broad range of projects—annual reports; posters; brochures; logo-types and symbols; corporate, retail and restaurant identity; exhibition design; and architectural signage. Douglas G. Harp considers himself most fortunate to have studied at Yale with Rudolph de Harak, Alvin Eisenman, Armin Hofmann, Paul Rand and Bradbury Thompson. He now teaches graphic design at the New York State College of Ceramics at Alfred University. His work has won recognition in the U.S. and Europe, and was recently included in the Moscow Triennial, *Man, Nature, Society.*

Harp and Company

Graphic identity, store signage, stationery and applications for Anthony Joseph the Store for Men, Corning, New York. Designers, (Logo and Components) Douglas G. Harp; (Components) Michelle M. Lockwood, Linda E. Wagner.
▼ ▶

AnthonyJoseph
THE STORE FOR MEN

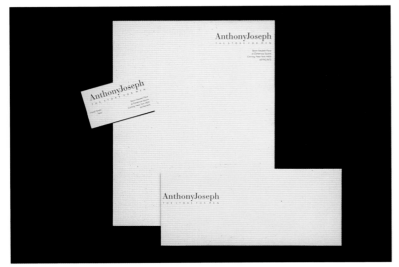

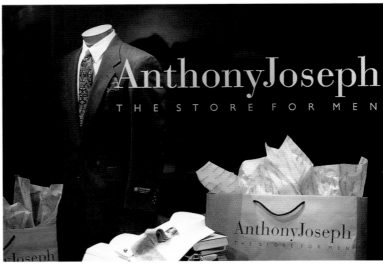

Chip chart design inaugurating a new collection of unique papers from around the world, for Mohawk Paper Mills, Cohoes, New York. Designers, Douglas G. Harp, Linda E. Wagner.
▶

Benefits brochures for The NTC Group, Greenwich, Connecticut. The brochures are targeted to NTC Group top managers. Designers, Douglas G. Harp, William Lucas; Illustrator, Lonni Sue Johnson.
▼

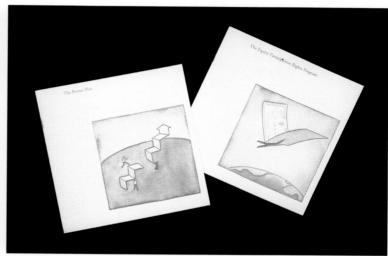

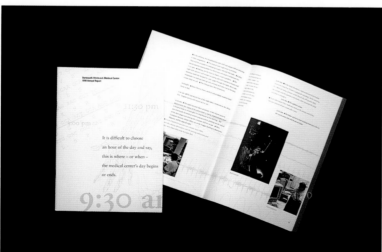

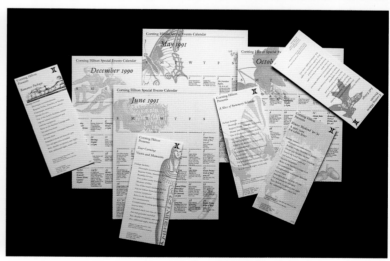

1989 annual report and capabilities brochure for Corning Incorporated, Corning, New York; Designers, Douglas G. Harp, Michelle M. Lockwood, with Corning Corporate Design staff. Photographer, Robert Barker; Writer, David Bellin.
▲

1990 annual report for Dartmouth-Hitchcock Medical Center, Lebanon, New Hampshire. Designers, Douglas G. Harp, Michelle M. Lockwood, Linda E. Wagner; Photographer, Jon Gilbert Fox; Writer, Megan M. Cooper.
▲

Christmas card design for the Corning Hilton, Corning, New York. Designer, Douglas G. Harp.
▶

Monthly calendars and weekend package announcements for the Corning Hilton, Corning, New York. Designers, Douglas G. Harp, Susan C. Harp, Michelle M. Lockwood.
▲

Graphic identity, including shopping bag, gift wrapping scheme, signage and store window design for Kids Delight clothing and toy store, Corning, New York. Designer, Douglas G. Harp.
▼

Graphic identity for the Children's Hospital at Dartmouth, Dartmouth-Hitchcock Medical Center, Lebanon, New Hampshire. The "D" is reproduced from a Dartmouth varsity letter sweater. Designer, Douglas G. Harp.
▶

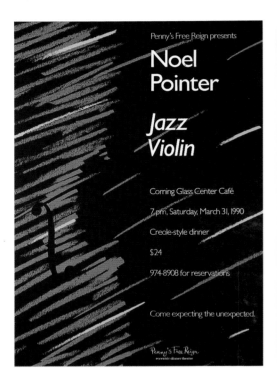

"Noel Pointer, Jazz Violin" poster for the Corning Glass Center Cafe, Penny's Free Reign dinner theatre. Designers, Douglas G. Harp, Michelle M. Lockwood.
▲

Graphic identity for Pazzo Restaurant, Corning, New York. The colors of the vegetables mimic those of the Italian flag. Designers, Douglas G. Harp, Susan C. Harp.
▶

Harp and Company

Graphic identity, main I.D. sign, and T-shirt design for Coyote Loco restaurant, Ithaca, New York. Designer, (Logo) Douglas G. Harp; (Components) Douglas G. Harp, Linda E. Wagner, Michelle M. Lockwood. ▼ ▶

Design for Greenkeeping Magazine, an environmental consumer's guide to practical, effective green products and services. For Green Alternatives, Inc., Rhinebeck, New York. Designers, Douglas G. Harp, Linda E. Wagner, Susan C. Harp. ▼

1991 season posters and ticket brochure for the Hangar Theatre, Ithaca, New York. Designers (Posters), Douglas G. Harp, Susan C. Harp; (Brochure) Linda E. Wagner; Illustrators, Douglas G. Harp, Susan C. Harp. ▲

Harp and Company

"SOS" poster design celebrating the 20th anniversary of Earth Day, for Corning Friends of the Earth, Corning, New York. Designers, Susan C. Harp, Douglas G. Harp; Screenprinting donated by Handone Studios, Rochester, New York.
▼

"Red Letter Day"poster design for the Corning Glass Center Cafe, Penny's Free Reign dinner theatre. Designers, Douglas G. Harp, Michelle M. Lockwood.
▶

Poster, T-shirt and program for "Reflections from the Crystal City," 1991 conference held by the Glass Art Society, Corning, New York. Designers, Linda E. Wagner, Douglas G. Harp.
◀ ▲

"Message to the Future" catalog and exhibition design for the New York State Artists Series, Herbert F. Johnson Museum of Art, Cornell University, Ithaca, New York. The artists' statements and captions are presented on pieces of paper grocery bags. Designers (Catalog), Douglas G. Harp, Michelle M. Lockwood; (Exhibition) Douglas G. Harp, Susan C. Harp.
▼ ▶

**Hornall Anderson
Design Works, Inc.**

1008 Western Avenue
6th Floor
Seattle, WA 98104
206/467-5800

John Hornall (seated)
and Jack Anderson,
Principals of Hornall
Anderson Design
Works, Inc.
▼

Western Washington
All British Field Meet,
poster design for
Puget Sound British
Motoring Society,
Seattle, Washington.
It's an annual exhibition
of British cars.
▲

"Friendship One"
exhibition and identity
for The Museum of Flight,
Seattle, Washington.
The Museum sponsored
the world record circum-
navigation flight attempt
to raise funds for children's
charities.
◄

Principals:
John Hornall
Jack Anderson
Year Founded: 1982
Size of Firm: 30
Key Clients:
Active Voice,
Airborne Express,
Asymetrix Corporation,
ATL,
Broadmoor Baker,
CHEF,
Food Services of
America,
Fred Hutchinson Cancer
Research Center,
Giro Sport Design,
Hillhaven Corporation,
Hogan's Market,
Holland America Line-
Westours, Inc.,
Intel Corporation,
K2 Corporation,
Lacroix,
Microsoft University,
Pane Di Paolo,
Porsche Cars North
America,
Print Northwest,
Raleigh Cycle Company
of America,
RF & A,
Starbucks Coffee
Company,
West One Bank,
Westin Hotels &
Resorts,
Windstar Cruises

Hornall Anderson Design Works

Being uncomfortable goes with the territory at Hornall Anderson Design Works – clients approving work that is a little beyond their comfort zone, suppliers being pushed to do more than they're comfortable with, and design teams who aren't comfortable with merely competent work. The result, as attested to by a client repeat rate of 80% in addition to hundreds of national and international design awards, is great work. The key to this success is hard work and teamwork, the Hornall Anderson approach to virtually every size and type of project. Clients are generally a part of this collaborative team process, and the bottom line for satisfied clients is always results. As one client observed on the outcome of his company's image and corporate identity update: "They feel quite strongly about the integrity of their design and don't compromise easily." "What would have taken two to three years with word of mouth was accomplished in a matter of months."

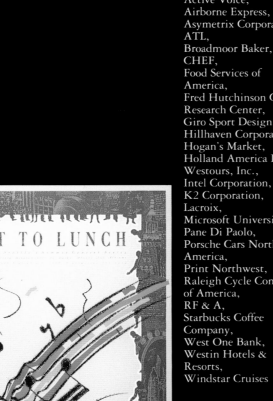

Promotional poster for Out-to-Lunch concert series. This is an annual outdoor concert program sponsored by the Downtown Seattle Association, Seattle, Washington.
▲

Commemorative poster for the Downtown Seattle Transit Project, for Metro, Seattle, Washington. The poster announced the completion of a new tunnel, improved bus system and above-ground improvements.
▶

**Hornall Anderson
Design Works, Inc.**

Banner system for City of Bellevue, Bellevue, Washington. The system includes 33 light standards, in series of four shapes in four sizes and eight color schemes. A steel collar ramp and nylon glides minimize wind load effects.
▼

Corporate identity for Hillhaven Corporation, Tacoma, Washington. The flower and hospital cross communicate the balance between medical care and family/residential care.
▼

Annual report for Hillhaven Corporation, Tacoma, Washington, a long term health care company.
▼

HILLHAVEN

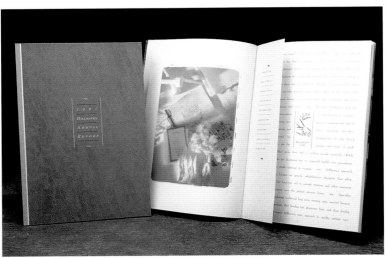

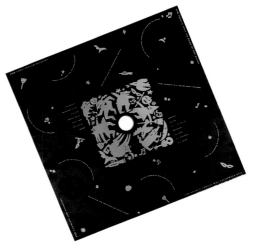

Here & Now magazine series and collateral materials for Roberts, Fitzmahan & Associates and Comprehensive Health Education Foundation, Seattle, Washington. The clients produce and market health education materials and curricula throughout the national school system.
▲

Halloween Ball invitation/poster design for Washington Software Association, Seattle, Washington.
◄

Product packaging design of Intel 387 DX Math CoProcessor, for Intel Corporation, Folsom, California.
▼

Identity program and graphics applications for Microsoft University, Redmond, Washington. The university is a satellite program developed by Microsoft Corporation to provide leading technical training for the micro-computer industry.
▼

Corporate identity and application for Active Voice, Seattle, Washington. The client is a telecommunications/call processing firm.

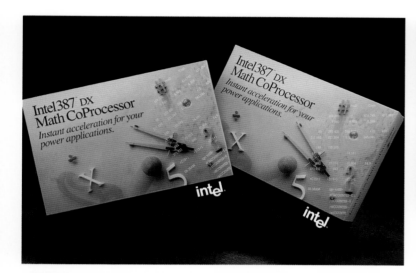

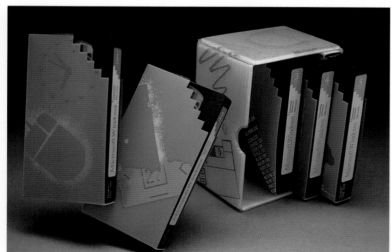

Brand identity and packaging design of HotLine software products, for General Information, Seattle, Washington.
◀

**Hornall Anderson
Design Works, Inc.**

Product line catalog for
Diadora athletic shoes,
Kent, Washington.
▼

Brand identity for
Eaglemoor golf attire
and accessories, Seattle,
Washington.
▼

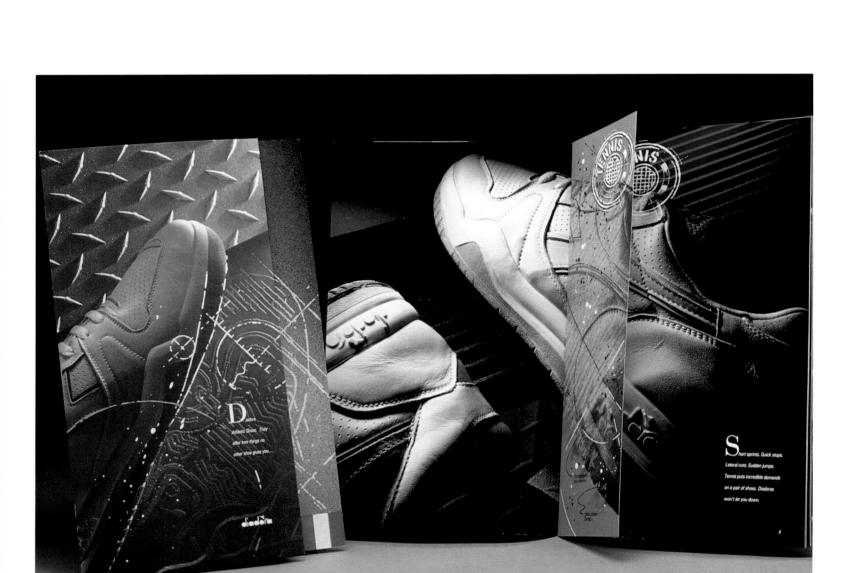

K2 8.3 Xtreme
brand/product identity
and graphics applications
for K2 Corporation,
Vashon, Washington.
▼ ▶

Brand identity and
hang tag design for
Dégage jeans, Seattle,
Washington.
▼

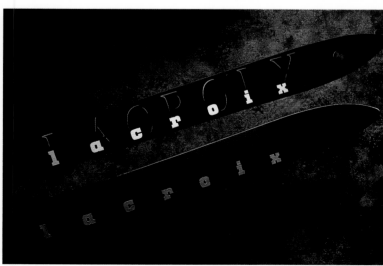

Ski graphics and promo-
tional brochure/poster for
Lacroix skis, France.
◀

80

**Hornall Anderson
Design Works, Inc.**

Clock tower, identity, environmental graphics and signage system for Canal Place 2000 complex, New Orleans, Louisiana.
▼

"Nobody Provides Better Service," Food Services of America's internal quality identity, Seattle, Washington.
◀

1992 promotional calendar for Food Services of America, Seattle, Washington.
▼

Corporate and brand identity and product packaging for Food Services of America, Seattle, Washington.
▶

Identity and package design for Italia restaurant, Seattle, Washington. Italia is an authentic Italian restaurant, deli and bakery that is also an urban gathering place and art gallery.
▼

Brand identity and package design for The Broadmoor Baker, Seattle, Washington. The client has expanded to more than seven varieties of quality bread products.
▼

Identity for Rikki Rikki restaurant, Kirkland, Washington.
◄

Retail identity and promotion designs for Hogan's Market of Puget Sound Marketing Corporation, Puyallup, Washington.
▼

Retail identity program for Tradewell Stores, Seattle, Washington.
◄

Alexander Isley Design

361 Broadway
Suite 111
New York, NY 10013
212/941-7945

Left to right:
Alexander Knowlton,
Barbara Sullivan, Philip
Bratter, Alexander Isley,
principal (pointing),
David Albertson, LaTanya
Autry, Kay Schuckhart.
▼

Promotion kit design
for Stat Store Publishing,
an output service bureau,
New York, New York.
The slipcase is the size of
a Mac disk for easy stor-
age and reference. Art
Director and Designer,
Alexander Isley.
▼

Poster and catalog designs
for the 1989 New Music
America Festival, for
the Brooklyn Academy
of Music. The face was also
used on T-shirts
and masks. Art Director,
Alexander Isley; Designer,
Alexander Knowlton.
▲ ▼

Principal:
Alexander Isley
Year Founded: 1988
Size of Firm: 7
Key Clients:
Advertising
Photographers
of America,
American Lung
Association,
American Museum of
the Moving Image,
Archaeological Institute
of America,
Brooklyn Academy
of Music,
Forbes, Inc.,
Giorgio Armani,
International Typeface
Corporation,
J&B Scotch,
Little, Brown Publishers,
McCaffrey and McCall
Advertising,
MTV Networks,
Nickelodeon,
PepsiCo.,
Spy Magazine,
Warner Bros. Records

Alexander Isley Design

"Thinking the Good Thought" poster design promoting a lecture by Alexander Isley, for the Maryland Institute College of Art, Baltimore, Maryland. Art Director and Designer, Alexander Isley.

▲

Black-and-white and color price lists for Stat Store. Art Director and Designer, Alexander Isley.

▼

Humor is a key to effective communication, Alexander Isley says, and it is present in virtually everything he designs. Even the simplest restaurant logo has wit. It's perhaps fitting that a recent project has been the book design of a tribute/history of the nation's most famous humor magazine, MAD. The former art director of *Spy* Magazine and designer at M&Co., Isley has, in a short space of time, built a succesful practice on the premise that the most effective message is usually the most unexpected one. Yet, not all his solutions are visual jokes or graphic puns. Through a graphic process of free play and serious conceptualizing, ideas are born that attract the reader or viewer and convey a message. This approach has earned him an eclectic list of clients that, in addition to MAD, includes Giorgio Armani and *Gazeta Wyborcza*, Poland's Solidarity newspaper, who have little in common except a need for intelligent design that provides an extra spark of dimension to both commōn and uncommon communications.

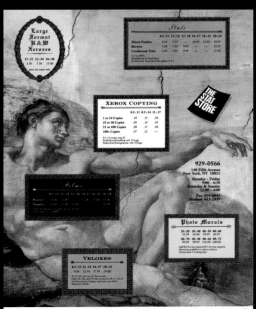

Alexander Isley Design

Graphic identity for Mesa Grill, a restaurant featuring southwestern food, New York, New York. The program includes design for menus, matchbooks, exterior signage and interior restroom signage. Art Director, Alexander Isley; Designer, Alexander Knowlton.
◀ ▶

Mesa Grill postcard series. Each features a favorite recipe of the restaurant's chef. Art Director, Alexander Isley; Designer, Alexander Knowlton.
▶

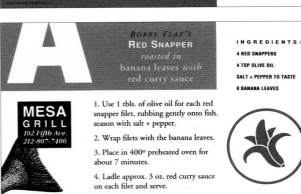

Catalog/brochure design for Choco-Logo, Inc., Buffalo, New York. The brochure was bound in the middle to yield two booklets: stock item chocolates, and custom chocolates. Art Director and Writer, Alexander Isley; Designer, Alexander Knowlton; Photographer, Jim Bush.
▶

**Alexander Isley
Design**

Identity and Packaging program for A/X: Armani/Exchange, for Giorgio Armani, Italy. The designers worked with Armani's agency Weiss, Whitten, Carroll, Stagliano to create everything from a logo for Armani Jeans to in-store signage, labels, shopping bags, gift boxes and wrap. Art Director, Alexander Isley; Designers, Tim Convery, Alexander Knowlton, Bruno Nesci. ▼

"Hallowe'en: Trick or Treat", book design for Clarkson N. Potter Publishers, New York, New York. Half of the book is printed upside down to create two parts, "Trick" and "Treat" and provide for two front covers. Art Director, Alexander Isley; Designer, Kay Schuckhart. ►

**Alexander Isley
Design**

Logo design for the American Museum of the Moving Image, Astoria, New York. The museum is devoted to the history and development of film and video. Art Director and Designer, Alexander Isley; Illustrator, Kam Mak.
▶

Program guides for The American Museum of the Moving Image. Art Director, Alexander Isley; Designer, Barbara Sullivan.
▼

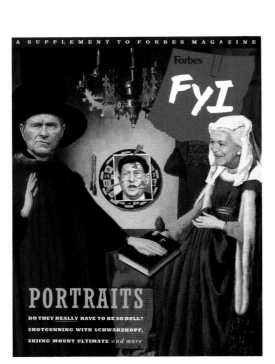

"Portraits", editorial design from issue of *Forbes FYI*, a quarterly publication that the studio produces for Forbes, Inc. Art Director, Alexander Isley; Designer, Kay Schuckart. Illustrator, Paul Bachem.
▲

Promotional brochure / media kit for *Gazeta Wyborcza*, the largest daily newspaper in Poland. The studio created a design that could be produced and printed in-house by the clients. The headline reads, "The Place to Say It." Art Director and Designer, Alexander Isley; Writer, Lisa Friedman.
◀

Cover and spread design for *Spy* Magazine, New York, New York. Isley was the first full time Art Director for the publication. Art Director, Alexander Isley; Designers, Alexander Knowlton, Catherine Gilmore-Barnes.

▼

Communication kit design for *Spy* Magazine. For use by ad sales staff, the kit encourages readers with a quarter for a call, a stamp for a letter, and a button advertising the magazine. Art Director and Designer, Alexander Isley.

►

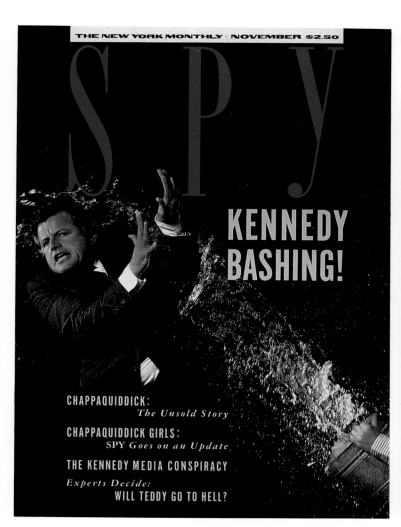

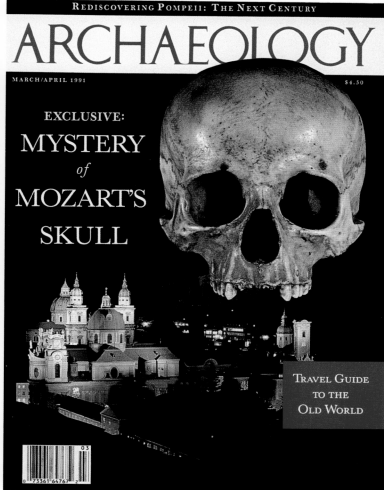

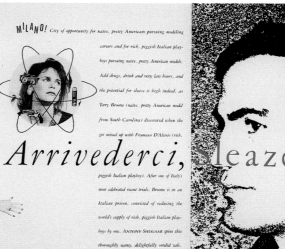

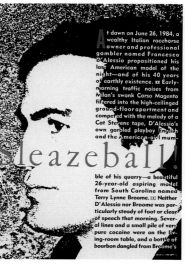

Redesign and continuing art direction for *Archaeology* Magazine, for the Archaeological Institute of America, Boston, Massachusetts. Art Director, Alexander Isley; Designer, Kay Schuckhart.

▲

"Spy High", book for Dolphin/Doubleday Publishers, New York, New York. Art Director, Alexander Isley; Designer, Barbara Sullivan.

◄

Alexander Isley Design

Bidding kit for Brooklyn Academy of Music Auction. The designers created a cover that fit over a standard clipboard. A pen and auction paddle were included. The inserts were prepared on a Mac and quick-printed the day of the auction. Art Director and Writer, Alexander Isley; Designer, Lynette Cortez.
▶

At first glance, it is obvious that the *Mad* offices at 485 Madison Avenue are not like those of any other business. The first clue is that they are on the thirteenth floor, a numeration that is actually deleted in most high-rise commercial buildings. The front door looks like any other, but a tiny label stuck below the mail slot reads: "Plastic Man entry." Choosing the normal route and opening the door, one enters a small vestibule that, with its several worn vinyl chairs and beige paint job, could pass for any neglected waiting room, except that the space is dominated by a life-size bronze statue of Alfred E. Neuman in a military

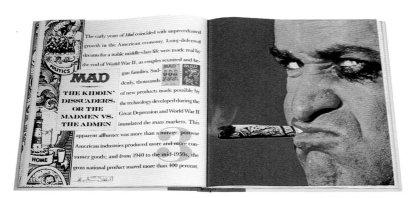

Book design, "Completely MAD: A History of the Comic Book and Magazine," for Little, Brown and Company, Boston, Massachusetts. The 216-page book celebrates the history of MAD on the magazine's 40th anniversary. The design includes a timeline consisting of each of 300 covers throughout the book. The designers also created a promotional fez for a booksellers convention. Art Director, Alexander Isley; Designer, Lynette Cortez.
◀ ▲ ▶

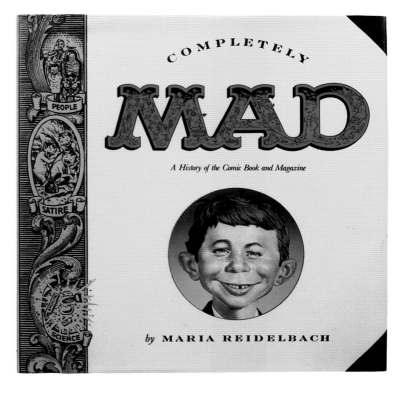

Alexander Isley Design

Design of the "APA Awards Book One," for the Advertising Photographers of America, New York, New York. Divider pages were created using details from the award-winning photographs. The cover type was silkscreened on clear vinyl. Art Director, Alexander Isley; Designer, Barbara Sullivan; Editor, Jill Bossert.
▼

CD and cassette packaging for "Dance Raja Dance, the music of Vijaya Anand" for David Byrne and Luaka Bop Records, New York, New York. Art Director, Alexander Isley; Designer, Alexander Knowlton; Illustrator, Paul Bachem.
▲

Logo for Weiss, Whitten, Carroll, Stagliano Inc. Advertising, New York, New York. Art Director, Alexander Isley; Designer, Philip Bratter.
▼

WEISS, WHITTEN, CARROLL, STAGLIANO INC.

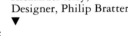

Weathervane promotional piece for Levine, Huntley, Schmidt and Beaver advertising agency, New York. To reach potential clients in the dairy industry, the designers created a series of custom weathervanes featuring LHS&B initials. Each piece came in a cow-patterned box. Art Director, Alexander Isley; Designer, Carrie Leeb.
◄

201 East 50th Street
New York, NY 10022
212/572-2363

Chip Kidd; Photography, Geoff Spear.
▼

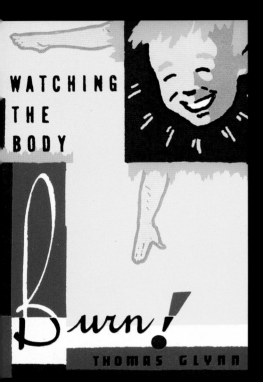

Watching the Body
Burn, by Thomas Glynn,
1989, jacket design for
Alfred A. Knopf, New
York, New York. Art
Director and Illustrator,
Chip Kidd.
▲

Principal:
Chip Kidd
Year Founded: 1964
Size of Firm: 1
Key Clients:
Alfred A. Knopf,
Bantam Doubleday
Dell,
Elektra Nonesuch
Records,
Farrar Straus Giroux,
HarperCollins,
William Morrow

Chip Kidd

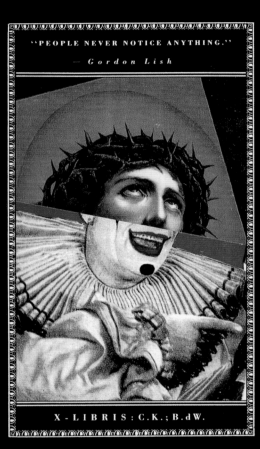

AIGA Book Show
1992 Call-For-Entries
("People Never Notice
Anything...") design
for AIGA National,
New York, New York.
Designers, Chip Kidd,
Barbara de Wilde;
Illustrator, Chip Kidd.
▲

Various adaptations of
the Borzoi dog logo for
Alfred A. Knopf, New
York, New York. The
five-legged creature at
the bottom appeared
on the book *Geek Love*,
a novel about freaks.
Designer, Chip Kidd.
▶

Five Years ago book jacket design took another of its periodic turns from an emphasis on simple, elegant, if not eclectic typography to a kind of flea market clutter. Chip Kidd, who has worked, almost exclusively, for over five years for Alfred A. Knopf since graduating from Pennsylvania State University, is the chief exponent of what might best be called the graphic non sequitur: a juxtaposition of disparate visual minutiae and iconography into a comprehensible entity. Kidd's images force the reader to experience, as well as read or view the message. Contrary to tradition, a book jacket or cover which has been thought of as a mini-poster is, in Kidd's hands, a collection of varied forms— from unabashedly stark to subversively subtle. The meaning of the book becomes subsumed under layers of engaging visual clues. Drawing much of his raw material from found and borrowed artifacts, Kidd creates alluring symbolic collages which, in concert with formalized letterforms or primitive scrawls, crystallize the more abstract aspects of text. Designed for the sophisticated reader, Kidd's jackets are meant to be decoded for maximum effect. By combining an acerbic wit with references from Pop and Punk art as well as the vernacular, he has developed a distinct graphic language that transcends the conventions of packaging while enlivening form.

Brazzaville Beach, by
William Boyd, 1991,
jacket design for William
Morrow, New York,
New York. The narrator
of the book smokes an
obscure brand of cigarettes.
Designer, Chip Kidd.
▼

Cover design of *The
Tax Inspector*, a novel by
Peter Carey, for Alfred
A. Knopf, New York,
New York. Art Director,
Carol Devine Carson;
Designer, Chip Kidd;
Photographer, Robert
Morrow.
▼

*The Actual Adventures of
Michael Missing*, stories by
Michael Hickins, 1991,
jacket design for Alfred A.
Knopf, New York,
New York. Designer,
Chip Kidd; Illustrator,
Charles Burns.
▼

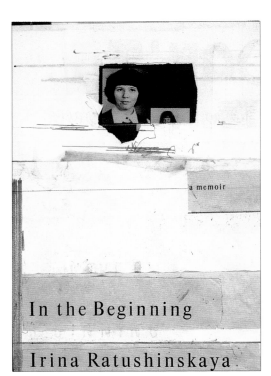

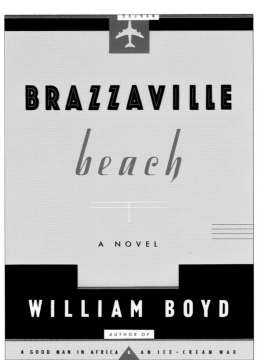

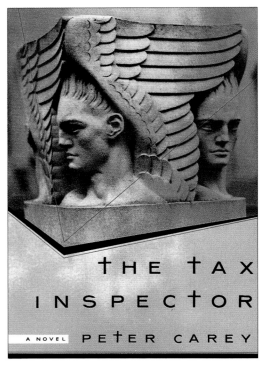

In the Beginning, memoirs
by Irina Ratushinskaya,
1991, jacket design
for Alfred A. Knopf,
New York, New York.
Designer and Collagist,
Chip Kidd.
▲

The Green Dark, poems
by Marie Ponsot, jacket
design for Alfred A.
Knopf, New York,
New York. Designer and
Photographer, Chip Kidd.
▶

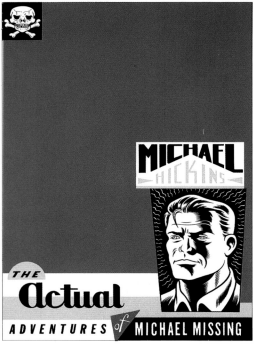

GEEK LOVE ◄

Handlettered jacket title
and cover design for
Geek Love, a novel by
Katherine Dunne,
for Alfred A. Knopf,
New York, New York.
Designer And Letterer,
Chip Kidd.

A

H A N D B O O K

F O R

D R O W N I N G

STORIES BY

D A V I D   S H I E L D S

**The American Replacement
of Nature**: William Irwin Thompson
The Everyday Acts and Outrageous Evolution of Economic Life

The American Replacement of Nature, by
William Irwin Thompson,
1991, jacket design for
Doubleday Currency,
New York, New York.
Designers, Chip Kidd,
Barbara de Wilde.
▲

*A Handbook for
Drowning*, stories by
David Shields, 1991,
jacket design for Alfred
A. Knopf, New York,
New York. Designers,
Chip Kidd, Barbara
de Wilde; Photographer,
David Barry.
◄

Cover, contents and
feature spread on linoleum,
design proposals for ID
Magazine redesign, 1991,
for ID Magazine, New
York, New York.
Designers, Chip Kidd,
Barbara de Wilde.

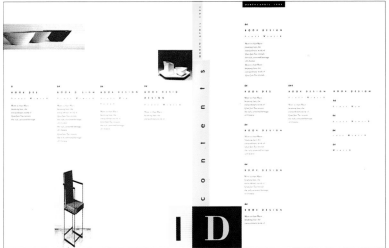

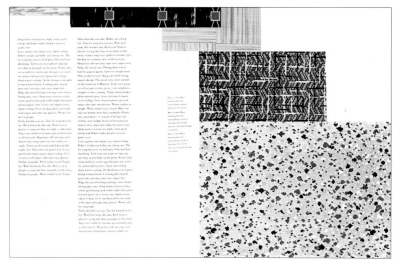

Invitation design for Committee for Lesbian and Gay Studies fund-raising evening, for CLAGS, New York, New York. Designer, Chip Kidd; Photographer, Geoff Spear.

▼

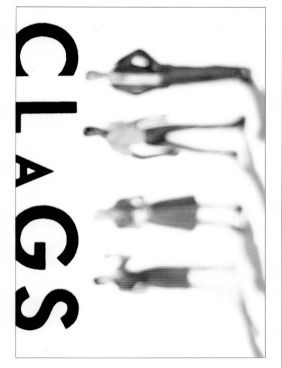

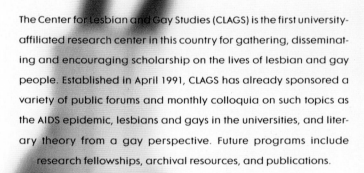

The Center for Lesbian and Gay Studies (CLAGS) is the first university-affiliated research center in this country for gathering, disseminating and encouraging scholarship on the lives of lesbian and gay people. Established in April 1991, CLAGS has already sponsored a variety of public forums and monthly colloquia on such topics as the AIDS epidemic, lesbians and gays in the universities, and literary theory from a gay perspective. Future programs include research fellowships, archival resources, and publications.

THE EXECUTIVE COMMITTEE

Martin Duberman, Director

Cheryl Clarke, Chairperson

Joseph Wittreich, Treasurer

Marcellus Blount, Jay Harper, Beverly Horton, Esther Katz, Seymour Kleinberg, Don Mengay, Sylvia Molloy, Vivien Ng, Jeff Nunokawa, Samuel Phillips, Amanda Prosser, Althea Smith, Alisa Solomon, Randolph Trumbach, Ellen Zaltzberg.

All You Who Sleep Tonight, poems by Vikram Seth, 1990, jacket design for Alfred A. Knopf, New York, New York. Designer, Chip Kidd; Photographer, Anton Stokowski.
▼

Logo mark for AIGA Book Show 1992, for AIGA National, New York, New York. Designers, Chip Kidd, Barbara de Wilde.
▶

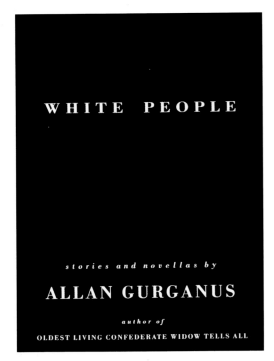

White People, stories by Allan Gurganus, 1991, jacket design for Alfred A. Knopf, New York, New York. Designer, Chip Kidd.
▲

Darling, by William Tester, 1992, jacket design for Alfred A. Knopf, New York, New York. Designer, Chip Kidd.
▼

Grey Is The Color of Hope, by Irina Ratushinskaya, jacket design for Alfred A. Knopf, New York, New York. Art Director, Carol Devine Carson; Designer, Chip Kidd.
▼

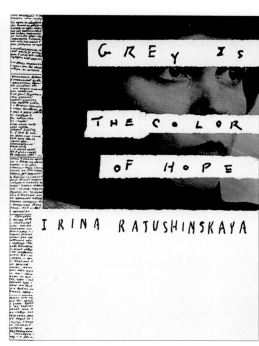

My Hard Bargain, stories by Walter Kirn, 1990, jacket design for Alfred A. Knopf, New York, New York. Designer and Photographer, Chip Kidd.
◄

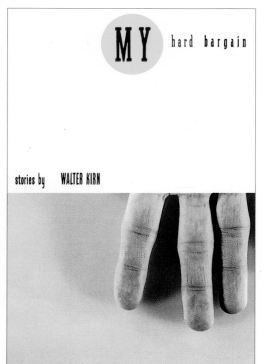

Kosh/Brooks Design

6671 Sunset Boulevard
#1574-A
Hollywood, CA 90028
213/465-9919

Kosh is on the left and
Larry Brooks is on the
right.
▼

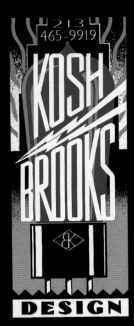

Logo design,
Kosh Brooks Design,
Hollywood, California.
Designers,
Kosh, Larry Brooks.
▲

"MGM: When The Lion
Roars," animated television
main title logo for
Turner Broadcasting and
Point Blank Productions,
Atlanta, Georgia and
Hollywood, California.
Designer, Kosh.
◄

Principals:
Kosh
Larry Brooks
Year Founded: 1989
Size of Firm: 5
Key Clients:
Atlantic Records,
Capital Records,
Champion Papers
International,
Chrysalis Records,
Elektra Records,
EMI Records,
MCA Records, Inc.,
MGM/UA,
Turner Broadcasting,
Warner Bros. Records

Kosh/Brooks Design

Kosh/Brooks Art
Director's Ponytail
self-promotional
Christmas gift in a
limited edition. Made
from "100% human
art director's hair."
The appropriate hair
color was sent to each
recipient. Designers,
Kosh, Larry Brooks.
▼

Kosh/Brooks Design has gained attention
—notoriety in fact – in the music industry
for the team's award-winning art direction
and design. This reputation is a result
of the firm's commitment to developing
a strong personal involement with artists and
management, guiding them from the initial concept
through every stage of a project's creative process.
This involvement leads ultimately to album cover
designs which not only perk consumer's curiosity with
their visual impact, but also supports an artistic
collaboration between the designers and clients that
impacts on sales. Principals Kosh and Larry Brooks
began their association in the mid-'80s, forming
Kosh/Brooks in 1989. Their long history of work
with the cream of the British rock bands such as
The Beatles, The Who, and The Rolling Stones, has
garnered three Grammy awards for design and art
direction. And they continue to be notoriously good.

Danny Elfman, "Music for a Darkened Theatre," CD cover design for MCA Records. Designer, Larry Brooks; Photographers, Dennis Keeley, David Norwood, Stuart Watson. ▼

Wire Train. MCA records. Designer, Larry Brooks; Photographer, Stuart Watson. ▼

The Gipsy Kings, "Mosaique", Elektra Records. Designers, Amy Dakos, Kosh; Illustrator, Amy Dakos. ▼

Kronos Quartet, "Winter Was Hard", Elektra Records. Designer, Kosh; Photographer, Michelle Clement.

Linda Ronstadt, "Cry Like A Rainstorm", Elektra Records. Designer, Kosh; Photographer, Robert Blakeman.

10,000 Maniacs, "In My Tribe", Elektra Records. Designer, Kosh. ▼

B.B. King, "There Is Always One More Time", MCA Records. Designer, Larry Brooks; Photographer, Hiroyuki Arakawa.

Mary's Danish, "Circa", Morgan Creek Records. Designer, Kosh. ▼

Kim Carnes, "Voyeur", EMI America Records. Designers, Kosh, Ron Larson; Photographer, Aaron Rapoport. ▼

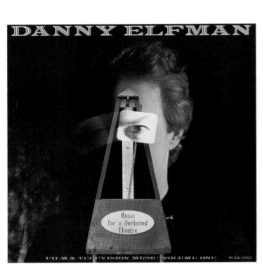

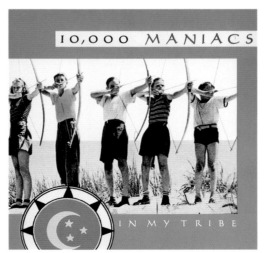

Kosh/Brooks Design

L.A. Guns, logo design, for Left Bank Management, Los Angeles, California. Designer, Kosh. ◀

Departmental signage designs for Cook-Fort Worth Children's Medical Center. Three out of a series of approximately 20 designs. Designer and Illustrator, Larry Brooks. ▶

PATIENT REGISTRATION

RADIOLOGY

PULMONARY & CARDIOLOGY

Spinal Tap, "Break Like the Wind," CD cover design and promotional packaging including "extra long" box, for MCA Records, Inc., Universal City, California. Designers, Kosh, Larry Brooks; Photographer, Peter Darley Miller. ▲

Slaughter, "The Wild
Life," CD packaging,
point-of-purchase and
merchandising materials
for Chrysalis Records,
New York, New York.
Designers, Kosh,
Larry Brooks.
◀ ▼

Mary's Danish
"American Standard,"
record album poster
design for Morgan Creek
Records, Los Angeles.
Designer, Kosh;
Photography,
Tommy Fecske.
▲

"In the Groove,"
promotional booklet and
spreads illustrating Groove
paper, for Champion
International, Stamford,
Connecticut. Designers and
Illustrators, Kosh,
Larry Brooks; Copywriter,
John Timpane.
▼

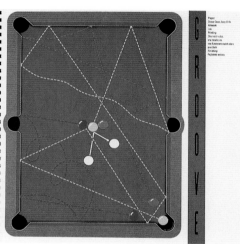
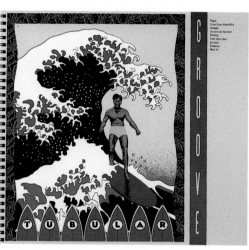

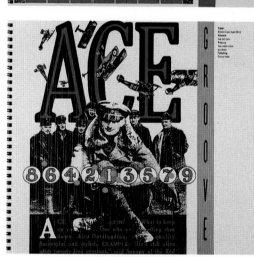

Walt Disney Mini Classics, logo design for a line of re-released Disney animated films on video, for Buena Vista, Burbank, California. Designer, Kosh.
◄

Cars and Stars, logo design for a line of trading cards displaying classic cars and their celebrity owners, for Machine Age, Los Angeles, California. Designer, Kosh.
▼

Publication design of The Workbook, California edition, a resource book for the graphic arts industry. This edition was designed as an original board game called "The Gender Trap" based on the volume's theme: Men and Women. Designers, Kosh, Larry Brooks; Illustrators, Brian Cronin, Kosh, Larry Brooks.
►

"The Origin and Evolution of the Tailfin, or The Benefit of Natural Selection," Benefit paper promotional book for Champion International Corporation, Stamford, Connecticut. Designers, Kosh, Larry Brooks, Amy Dakos.
▼

Eleven, "Awake in a
Dream," CD packaging
for Morgan Creek Records,
Los Angeles, California.
Designer and Illustrator,
Kosh.
▼

Vidal Sassoon Salons
"Turnstyle" logo design
promoting a salon
cut that can be styled
two completely different
ways. Designer,
Larry Brooks.
◀

Steppenwolf, "Born to
be Wild" Retrospective,
CD packaging for
MCA Records, Inc.,
Universal City,
California. Designer,
Larry Brooks.
▶

Chicago, "Twenty One,"
album cover, CD,
cassette, and promotion
copies, for Warner Bros.
Records, Los Angeles,
California. Designers,
Kosh, Larry Brooks;
Illustrator, Larry Brooks.
▲

Jennifer Morla is president and creative director of Morla Design Inc., in San Francisco. Recent projects include animation for MTV, interior design programs for Levi Strauss, Swatch Watch designs, and extensive identity campaigns for experimental art organizations and museums. Ms. Morla has received awards from the American Institute of Graphic Arts, the American Center for Design, and has been featured in *Communication Arts* magazine. In addition to teaching Senior Graphic Design at California College of Arts and Crafts, she is also a featured speaker and frequent national show juror.

Not An Essay, Just Some Design Thoughts

Jennifer Morla

Taking risks is the key to unlocking creativity.

Design is seductive propaganda.

Effective design is layered communication.

Design does not exist in a vacuum. Design is influenced by and influences contemporary society.

The conceptual design process can be articulated through action, words and images. All can have equal value and equal impact.

New ideas are the product of learning to yearn.

Design is not solely a marketing device that supports consumerism. It can be a communicator of dissent. It can market ideology. It can effect change.

The collaborative process is the joy of design.

As our knowledge of environmental issues expands, increased access to conservation measures implies a greater responsibility to use them.

The truest form of waste management is questioning and evaluating the need for any piece of print communication.

Question "graphic" as an adjective of design. As "graphic designers" we create environments, design furniture, animate videos, art direct film, pattern clothing; all forms of expression and problem solving not limited to the traditional two-dimensional definition.

As a profession, we are strong, both economically and influentially. We can make design a part of the vernacular by having representation in our dictionaries, our libraries, our museums.

Liska & Associates, Inc.

676 North St. Clair
Suite 1550
Chicago IL 60611
312/943-4600

Steven Liska.
▲

Capabilities brochure for
Magnum Photos, Inc.,
New York, New York.
Designers, Kim Nyberg,
Steven Liska.
◄ ▲

Principals:
Steven Liska
Year Founded: 1979
Size of Firm: 8
Key Clients:
American Society of
Plastic and
Reconstructive Surgeons,
Ameritech,
Chicago Mercantile
Exchange,
Chicago Symphony
Orchestra,
Houghton-Mifflin
Company,

IBM,
International Events
Group,
International Paper
Company,
Kemper Financial
Services, Inc.,
Magnum Photos, Inc.,
Mohawk Paper Mills,
NEC Technologies, Inc.,
Potlatch Corporation,
Scott, Foresman &
Company,
Underwriters Laboratories

Liska &
Associates, Inc.

A t Liska and Associates, the goals of every project are to involve and intrigue, inform and educate. "To do this the firm makes sure that the visual and verbal solutions support the client's marketing objectives and still have a unique, individual voice," explains principal Steve Liska. The firm's work is produced with a sense of informal community and utilizes sense, wit, aesthetics and production values to solve problems. Having stayed relatively small, they can remain very involved and service-oriented with each project. "We are neither trendy nor conservative," Liska comments, "we use our brains more than our scanner." The result is work that illuminates verbal ideas with visual clarity. Delineating every project—from a single logo design to multi-layered identity systems—to its most precisely focused function, is what enables this Chicago firm to successfully complement complex ideas with simple graphic solutions.

Miraweb/Miragloss
paper promotion for
International Paper.
Designers, Marcia
Lausen, Heidi Fieschko,
Steven Liska; Photographer, Laurie Rubin.
▲ ▶

Brochure design for NEC Technologies, Inc., Wood Dale, Illinois. The brochure describes the capabilities of a new line of color-adjustable computer monitors for the Mac. Designers, Kim Nyberg, Steven Liska; Photographer, Steve Grubman.
▼

Liska & Associates, Inc.

CD-sized brochure design for NEC Technologies, Inc. Designers, Brock Haldeman, Richard Taylor, Steven Liska.
►

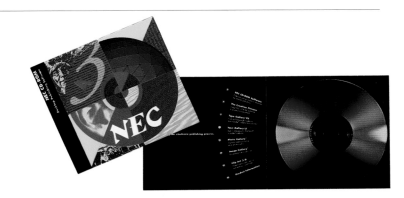

Breakthrough display solutions for the Macintosh computer. Presenting the 15", 17" and 21" NEC MultiSync FG Display Solutions for the complete Macintosh® II family and the powerful new Macintosh Quadra™ series of computers. MultiSync FG monitors combine features that complement the Macintosh computer and advanced screen performance for brighter, sharper, more accurate images. The MacFG Color Display Interface card,

engineered in conjunction with Radius,™ gives you flexible display capabilities seamlessly integrated with each of the MultiSync FG monitors. Together, the monitors and display interface create a total display solution that will meet virtually any application need.

Larger, more accurate images. Each monitor in the new FG line features a significantly larger active display area. The addi-

tional display area is a function of larger screen size, of edge-to-edge images provided by NEC's FullScan™ capability and of the custom display modes resident in the MacFG™ Color Display Interface. That means you'll have no unused screen area between the image and the monitor bezel. Each FG monitor's flat square screen surface is flatter both horizontally and vertically, offering a much more consistent edge-to-edge image.

Unprecedented color accuracy. The MultiSync FG line also introduces NEC's revolutionary AccuColor™ Control System. The AccuColor Control System allows you to adjust on-screen colors to meet your individual needs and preferences. At last, you can have WYSIWYG color accuracy.

Advanced display performance for graphical applications. NEC MultiSync FG

display solutions offer breakthrough display capabilities that take full advantage of the Macintosh computer's extraordinary graphic abilities.

To begin with, larger displays put more information on-screen, providing a larger desktop. And on NEC's flat square screen surfaces, images appear flat with less distortion at the edges. The high-contrast screen surface

improves focus and displays colors more vibrantly. An advanced shadowmask made of heat resistant Invar alloy enables increased brightness with no loss of focus. And higher refresh rates produce flicker-free images, especially important for the white screen backgrounds found in many business applications.

MultiSync 4FG, 5FG and 6FG monitors also feature microprocessor-based memory and

digital controls. These store preset and custom graphics modes to automatically size and center screen images, and allow you to control image size and position and on-screen color.

And NEC's exclusive ErgoDesign™ philosophy provides innovative comfort and ease of use features which can enhance your productivity dramatically.

The advanced, flat square MultiSync FG monitors are available separately or combined with the MacFG Color Display Interface card for a complete graphics solution. So whether you're configuring a new system or simply upgrading your monitor, NEC offers a high performance display solution designed specifically for your Apple® Macintosh computer.

Introducing the AccuColor Control System: an unprecedented advance in user-adjustable color accuracy. As a Macintosh user you know the value of color and the ability to manipulate it in today's computing environments. NEC's exclusive AccuColor Control System provides a revolutionary technological advance that

simplifies the process of manipulating on-screen color.

Simply revolutionary. The AccuColor Control System is NEC's device and application-independent color calibration system which is built-in on 4FG, 5FG and 6FG monitors. Accessed through the monitors' digital controls, it

enables you to adjust on-screen colors to meet your individual needs and preferences. With the AccuColor Control System you can separately adjust the monitor's red, green and blue color intensities in precise digital steps to optimize on-screen color to your preferred setting.

By putting the ability to adjust color within the monitor itself, no additional hardware or software is required and color settings within

your system can remain constant. With AccuColor, you don't have to change the color palette in your software or video board to change the color on your screen. And the AccuColor Control System automatically balances your on-screen color as you adjust brightness and contrast levels.

Match your screen color to just about anything. With the AccuColor Control

System, MultiSync FG monitors let you match on-screen colors to color reference systems. You can also match on-screen color to the hard copy color delivered by your color printer. Or by other monitors. Or simply adjust your display to the color you want to see. With this amazing advance in color accuracy, you can get the most out of 8-bit and 24-bit color capability.

Easy to use, too. The AccuColor Control System is also incredibly easy to use. You can hold a swatch of color from an output device or color reference guide up to the screen and use the digital control buttons to adjust the image and store your color settings in memory. Because it's done visually, you can match your screen color to virtually anything and your own eyes are the judge of accuracy.

Who needs AccuColor? If you use today's business productivity applications, you know that they're relying on color more than ever. And with AccuColor they can be more productive than ever. If you use desktop publishing or graphics applications, you know how important it is to match the color on your screen with the color you want printed. And for color prepress applications, AccuColor saves time, effort, frustration—and money—

by eliminating trial and error color adjustments and reducing rework costs. Or maybe you're just someone who wants more control over the colors on your display. The AccuColor Control System gives you that control.

Noir et Blanc on
Quintessence, paper
promotion for Potlatch
Paper Corporation,
Cloquet, Minnesota.
Designers, Anne
Schedler, Steven Liska.
▼

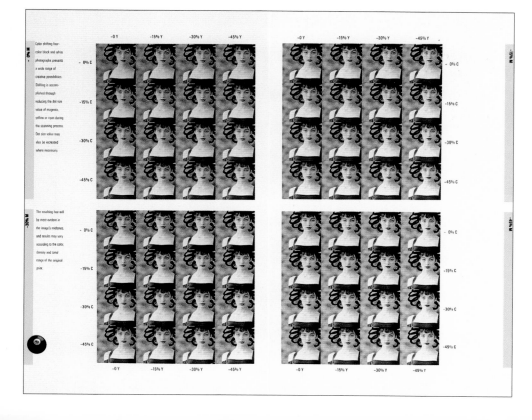

Liska & Associates, Inc.

A World Marketplace, capabilities brochure for the Chicago Mercantile Exchange. The text includes French and Japanese translations. Designers, George Wong, Bob Prow, Steven Liska; Photographers, Scott Morgan (cover), Tim Bieber (interior).

▼

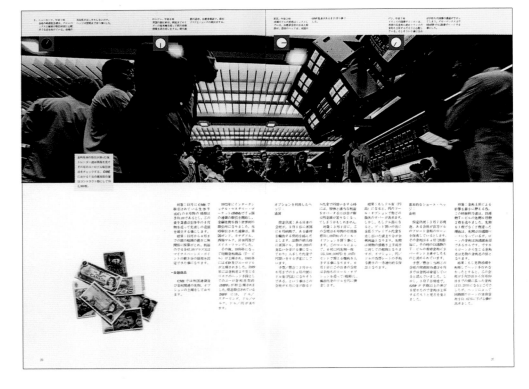

Poster designed from a panoramic image for the Chicago Mercantile Exchange. An image of the Exchange trading floor was also used as a double gatefold annual report cover. Designers, Bob Prow, Steven Liska; Photographer, Mark Segal.
▼

Chicago Mercantile Exchange annual report, 1988. Designer, Steven Liska; Illustrator, Alan Cober
▼

Logo identity for Globex division of the Chicago Mercantile Exchange.

Liska & Associates, Inc.

Miraweb/Miragloss paper promotion for International Paper, Memphis, Tennessee. Designers, Marcia Lausen, Heidi Fieschko, Steven Liska; Photographer, Laurie Rubin.
▼

Logo identity for Horticultural Design Limited, Lake Bluff, Illinois.
◄

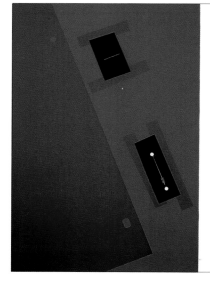

Brochure design for Active Graphics, Chicago, Illinois. Designers, Bob Cosgrove, Kim Nyberg.
▲

**Liska &
Associates, Inc.**

Logo design and graphic
identity for the American
Society of Aesthetic
Plastic Surgeons,
Arlington Heights,
Illinois.

◄

Logo identity for textile
designer Martin Rogers,
Chicago, Illinois.

►

MARTIN ROGERS

**Michael Mabry
Design**

212 Sutter Street,
San Francisco, CA 94108
415/982-7336

Poster design for
"Worldesign '92," the
Industrial Designers
Society of America
conference held every
four years which focuses
on design and global
issues. Designer,
Michael Mabry.
▼

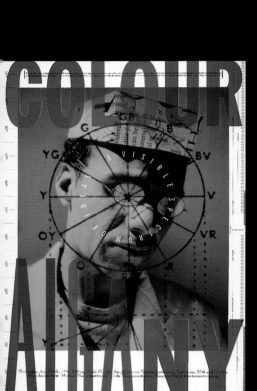

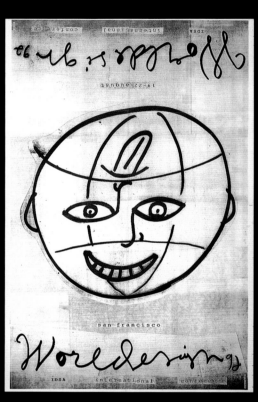

AIGA/NY poster
announcing a lecture on
color. Designers,
Michael Mabry, Margie
Chu; Photographer,
Michael Mabry.

Michael Mabry.
▶

Principal:
Michael Mabry
Year Founded: 1981
Size of Firm: 5
Key Clients:
Cole Weber,
Chronicle Books,
DDB Needham
Worldwide,
Foote Cone and Belding,
Friends of Photography,
HarperCollins,
Lunar Design,
Levi Strauss and Co.,
Mon Jardinet Ltd.,
Nike,
Random House,
San Francisco Focus
Magazine

Michael Mabry Design

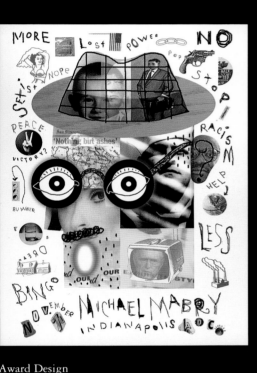

Michael Mabry likes to make things look simple, even if they are very complex—in his work, as well as his relationship with clients. It's less the lack of a bluechip education than a quality of naivete in his work, which draws people in at first glance. His design was described as "a union of things disparate and those strikingly alike. A balance kept by knowing just what is undeniably essential." What is essential to him is that he hits a nerve right off, but that with second and third glances, there is something deeper revealed. Not happy doing the same thing over and over, Mabry is continually exploring. He soaks up everything he sees, and sooner or later it surfaces in some shape or form in his work. Founded in 1981, Michael Mabry Design has remained a firm that is small (currently five) by staff numbers, but large in scope of ideas. With a focus recently on retail-related projects, the work varies stylistically from client to client; it is not intellectual. It is serious, but not up in the clouds. There is a humorous side to the work—fairly quirky and almost childlike— which is balanced with an intuitive sense of reserve. Mabry knows when he's hit the mark. And his second profession would be running a magazine stand.

Corporate identity for Lunar Design, a full service industrial and product design company. Designer, Michael Mabry.

Logo design for a division of DDB Needham Worldwide, focusing on children's advertising. Creative Director, David Jenkins; Designer, Michael Mabry.

Cover design and divider pages for Lunar Design's capabilities brochure. Designers, Michael Mabry, Peter Soe, Jr.; Photographers, Rick English, Michael Mabry.

Book design, cover and spreads for *American Illustration Ten*, published by Watson-Guptill, New York. Designer, Michael Mabry; Cover Illustrator, Gary Baseman.

Catalog design for the Untitled series of catalogs for the Friends of Photography, which showcase the work of various fine art photographers. Editor, David Featherstone; Designers, Michael Mabry, Margie Chu.

Corporate identity program for the Friends of Photography. Designers, Michael Mabry, Margie Chu. ▼

"Technical Series" brochure design for James H. Barry, fine lithographers of San Francisco. Designers, Michael Mabry, Margie Chu; Photographer, Michael Lamotte. ▶

Capabilities brochure design for James H. Barry. Designer, Michael Mabry; Photographer, Michael Lamotte. ▲

"Master of Ceremonies," logo design for McDougall Creative, a full-service producer of corporate communications events. Designer, Michael Mabry. ▼

Montage art. Designer, Michael Mabry; Photographers, Albert Watson, Sandra Haber, Scott Morgan, Thomas Heinser, Yuen, Henrik Kam; Illustrator, Josh Gosfield, Marvel Comics.

▶

SilverTab is a fashion forward line of Levi's for Men, ages 18-25. The redesign of the whole graphic identity system included outdoor advertising ads, Bloomingdale's mailer, point-of-purchase poster, spread and back cover of trade ad, bus shelter advertisements, and packaging design.

122

Package design for Mon Jardinet, Ltd. Designer, Michael Mabry.
▼

Logo design for Zim's Restaurants, "Home of the Zimburger since 1948." Designers, Michael Mabry, Peter Soe, Jr.; Illustrator, Steven Guarnaccia.
▶

Package design for Zélé, a beer refresher known in France as a panaché, created for the U.S. market. Designer, Michael Mabry.
▼

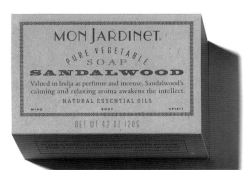

Michael Mabry Design

Consumer ad for Nike's Tensile Air, a new air comforting system in dress shoes. Art Directors, Jim Nevins, Michael Mabry; Designer, Michael Mabry; Photographer, Terry Heffernan. ▼

i.e. consumer ads. Art Director and Designer, Michael Mabry; Photographer, Brigitte Lacombe. ▼

[Gravity] *It's what's wrong with every pair of shoes you've ever owned.*

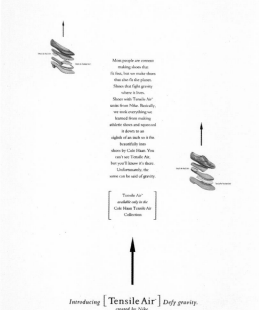

Introducing [Tensile Air] *Defy gravity.* created by Nike

i.e., trade catalog design. Designers, Michael Mabry, Margie Chu; Photographers, Brigitte Lacombe, Dan Langley. ▲

Visual identity program for Video/FX desktop video production equipment, for Digital F/X, Mountain View, California. Art Director, Clement Mok; Designers, Sandra Koenig, Clement Mok; Illustrator, Mick Wiggins.

Clement Mok designs, Inc.

Clement Mok designs, Inc.
600 Townsend Street
Penthouse
San Francisco, CA 94103
415/703-9900

Design for Apple QuickTime CD clip video library, for Apple Computer, Cupertino, California. The clip is one of 360-plus video sequences from the library. Art Director and Designer, Clement Mok; Art Director, Writer, Designer, Doris Mitsch; Producer, Clancy Nolan; Animators, Programmers, Clancy Nolan, Kevin Lyons.
▼

Clement Mok, principal of Clement Mok designs, Inc.
▼

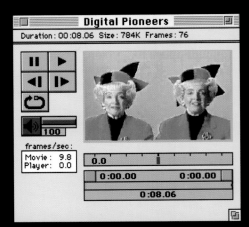

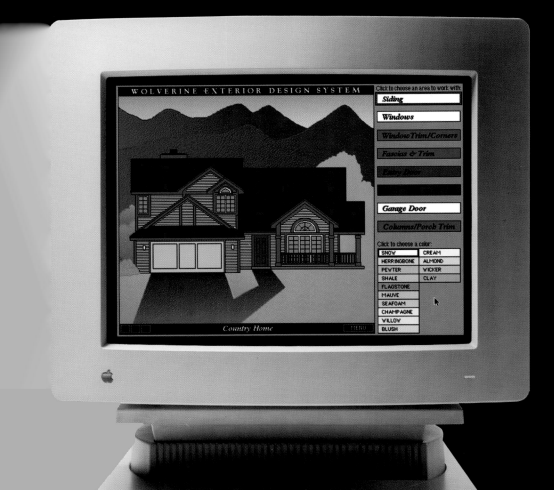

Interactive product catalog for Wolverine Exterior Systems, Detroit, Michigan. Art Director, Designer, Programmer, Doris Mitsch; Illustrator, John Widmer.
◄ ▲

Product brochure design
for TypeReader Software,
for Expervision, San
Francisco, California. Art
Director and Designer,
Clement Mok; Photog-
raphers, Michael Lamotte,
Tom Zimberoff.
▼

Principal:
Clement Mok
Year Founded: 1988
Size of Firm:18
Key Clients:
3Com,
Apple Computer,
Aldus,
Bennetton,
Brøderbund,
Caere Corporation,
CBS Entertainment,
Claris Corporation,
Connect,
DEC,
Everex,
Farallon Computing,
frogdesign,
Hallmark Cards,
Hewlett-Packard,
Macromedia,
Mirage Hotel & Casino,
Mayo Clinic,
Northern Telecom,
Pillar Corporation,
Revo Sunglasses,
Simpson Paper,
Sun Microsystems,
SuperMac Technologies,
TED2,
Walt Disney
Imagineering,
Wolverine

Clement Mok designs, Inc.

PRESENTING
TYPEREADER.

THE FIRST OCR
SOFTWARE THAT
CAN READ ANY
PAGE OF TYPE.

ExperVision

Cover illustration for
a series of manuals
about interface design
standards, for GO
Corporation, Redwood
City, California.
Illustrator, Clement Mok.
▶

Since its founding in early 1988, CMd has developed a unique expertise in explaining products and ideas that have never existed before—new tools, new concepts, and new paradigms for the way people think, work, learn and communicate. In a world where growing demands on people's time lead to shrinking spans of attention, the substance of a business message increasingly resides in images, symbols, and visual shorthand. Creating effective communication is, fundamentally, a strategic issue—a way to out-think, out-plan, and out-perform the competition. The right strategy results in competitive advantage, just as the right design inspires insights, evokes responses and, ultimately, transforms thought into action. This competitive drive is primarily the result of Clement Mok's tenure as creative director during the heyday of Apple Computer's formative years with Steve Jobs and John Sculley. The company's work spans diverse disciplines including print, animation, video, advertising, packaging, exhibit and computer interface design. CMd believes that design—its strategic planning, clear intention, and artful execution—can determine whether a product sells or gathers dust; whether an idea is understood or rejected; whether a vision is embraced or dismissed. CMd continues to make a vision of the future alive in the present, to make technical information digestible and understandable, and conveys lasting messages via ephemeral electronic media without dehumanizing the essence of what it means to be a person.

Visual identity program for REVOsunglasses, for REVO, Inc., Mountain View, California. Art Director, Clement Mok; Designers, Lori Nason, Jack Herr.
▼

Logo design for Pillar Corporation, Redwood City, California. Art Directors, Clement Mok, Sandra Koenig; Designer, Sandra Koenig.
▶

pīIIar

Rēvo

Clement Mok designs, Inc.

Software packaging system for Macromedia, San Francisco, California. Art Director, Clement Mok; Designers, Sandra Koenig, Dale Horstman, Nancy Bauch; Illustrator, Ron Chan. Production, Chuck Adsit.
▼

Logotype and visual identity for The Republic of Tea, Mill Valley, California. Art Director, Clement Mok; Designer, Nancy Bauch; Calligrapher, Georgia Deaver.
▶

The REPUBLIC of TEA

Interactive conference directory for the 2nd Annual Technology, Entertainment and Design Conference (TED2). Art Directors, Clement Mok, Doris Mitsch; Designers, Kevin Lyons, Clement Mok; Programmers, Peter Vanags, Kevin Lyons.
▼

Product demo for GO Corporation, Redwood City, California. Screen graphics are used with a pen-based computer technology. Art Director and Producer, Doris Mitsch; Designers, Doris Mitsch and Dale Horstman; Production and Illustrator, Michael Crumpton.
▼

Imagery from ad for Farallon Computing on Mac to PC Networking. Art Directors, Doris Mitsch, Clement Mok; Designer, Doris Mitsch.
▶

CD-Interactive family health and medical reference, for Interactive Ventures, Eagan, Minnesota. Art Director, Doris Mitsch; Designers, Doris Mitsch, Jennifer Anderson; Programmer and Animator, Clancy Nolan.
▲

Visual identity for
The Mirage Hotel and
Casino, for Mirage
Corporation, Las Vegas,
Nevada. Art Director,
Clement Mok; Designers,
Sandra Koenig, Clement
Mok, Dale Horstman;
Illustrator, Clement Mok.
▼

**Clement Mok
designs, Inc.**

Signage graphics for the
Land Pavilion, EPCOT
Center, for Walt Disney
Imagineering, Burbank,
California. Art Director,
Clement Mok; Designers,
Clement Mok, Kevin
Lyons.
▼

Video for Revo, Mountain
View, California. Art
Director and Producer,
Doris Mitsch; Designers,
Clement Mok, Doris
Mitsch, Lori Nason;
Animators, Chuck Adsit,
Doris Mitsch; Audio
Engineer, Steve Shapiro;
Camera and Production,
Eclipse Productions.
▼

An interactive CD-
ROM with reference
information on new
presentation techno-
logies, for Apple Pacific,
Cupertino, California.
Art Directors, Clement
Mok, Doris Mitsch;
Designers, Clement
Mok, Doris Mitsch,
Kevin Lyons; Audio
Engineer, Gary
Levenberg; Original
Music, Nick tenBlock;
Photographer,
Steve Underwood;
Programming, Medior.
▼

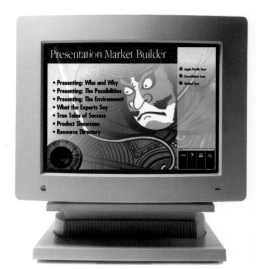

130

Screen and interface design for interactive guide to movies to video, for The Good Guides. Art Director, Clement Mok; Designer and Programmer, Bruce Charonnat. ▼

Interactive demo for Digital Equipment Corp.'s Client/Server Multimedia Products, Palo Alto, California. Art Directors, Clement Mok, Doris Mitsch; Writer, Doris Mitsch; Designers, Kevin Lyons, Clement Mok; Programming, Eneranalytic, Audio Engineer, Gary Levenberg; Music, Turtle Island Quartet; Illustrator, Ward Schumaker. ▼

Logo design for Connect Information System, Cupertino, California. Art Director and Designer, Clement Mok. ▼

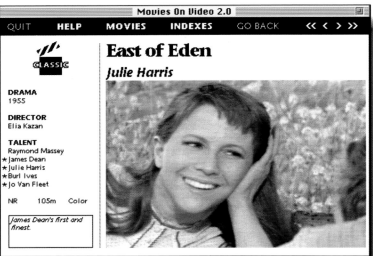

CONNECT

Imagery from ad on networking, for Farallon Computing, Emeryville, California. Art Director and Designer, Doris Mitsch. ◄

Apple Worldwide
Developer Conference
support materials,
for Apple Development
Group, Cupertino
California. Art Director,
Clement Mok; Designers,
Chuck Routhier,
Clement Mok, Lori Nason.
▼

**Clement Mok
designs, Inc.**

Design of exhibit booth
for 3Com Corporation,
Santa Clara, California.
Art Directors, Clement
Mok, Nancy Bauch;
Designer, Nancy Bauch,
Computer Modeling,
Chuck Adsit.
▼

Logo design for *Currency*
book series, for Doubleday
Books, New York. Art
Director, Clement Mok;
Designer, Nancy Bauch;
Prodution, Seth Bain.
◄

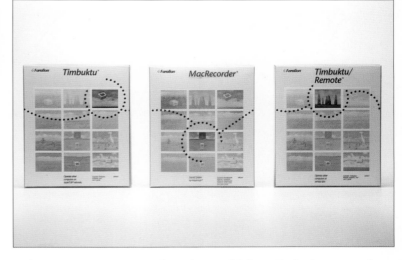

Packaging system
for Omnipage OCR-
Software, for Caere
Corporation, Los Gatos,
California. Art Director,
Clement Mok; Designers,
Chuck Routhier,
Clement Mok.
◄

Package design of Color
Calibrator, for SuperMac
Technologies, Mountain
View, California. Art
Director, Clement Mok;
Designer, Mark
Crumpacker.
▲

Packaging system for
Farallon Computing.
Art Director, Clement
Mok; Designers, Chuck
Routhier, Clement Mok;
Illustrator, Mark
Penberthy.
▲

Morla Design, Inc.

463 Bryant Street
San Francisco, CA 94107
415/543-6548

Jennifer Morla,
principal of Morla
Design, Inc.
▼

Poster design for the
Stanford Conference
on Design, for the
Stanford Alumni
Association, Stanford,
California. Designer
and Illustrator,
Jennifer Morla.
▼

One-color poster
designed for AIGA/San
Francisco to educate
the public and promote
individual action on
environmental issues.
Designers, Jennifer Morla,
Jeanette Aramburu.
▶

Poster design for the
San Francisco Museum
of Modern Art Lecture
Series, for AIGA/
San Francisco. The
image aggressively
interprets "The Radical
Response." Designers,
Jennifer Morla, Sharrie
Brooks; Photography,
Bybee Studios, A.R.T.
Lab; Illustrator, Jennifer
Morla.
▼

Principal:
Jennifer Morla
Year Founded: 1984
Size of Firm: 7
Key Clients:
American Institute of
Graphic Arts (AIGA),
Amnesty International,
Esprit de Corp,
Foote, Cone & Belding,
Goodby Berlin
& Silverstein,
Levi Strauss & Co.,
MTV Television,
The Mexican Museum,
San Francisco
International Airport,
San Francisco Museum
of Modern Art,
Simpson Paper
Company,
Swatch Watch,
Wells Fargo Bank,
Windham Hill Records

Morla Design

With a striking ability to pair elegance and wit with a distinctive sensibility for type and image, Morla Design, Inc. creates a body of work that successfully meets many design challenges. Formed in 1984 as a multi-faceted design firm offering creative services which encompass collateral, packaging, identity, logo, signage and interior architectural design, the firm has been instrumental in the image building of some of the country's largest and most visible corporations, building a strong reputation by creating successful and dynamic visuals for clients as diverse as Wells Fargo, Levi's, Amnesty International and Windham Hill Records. Whether creating an energized retail space in which to spark consumer purchasing, or lending typographic beauty to gourmet food packaging, Morla Design evolves design solutions tailored to attract their clientele's target audience. The firm's achievements in print, broadcast and architectural graphics have been honored in numerous competitions and publications, as well as receiving gold and silver medals from the New York and the San Francisco Art Directors Clubs with work represented in the permanent collections of the San Francisco Museum of Modern Art and the Library of Congress.

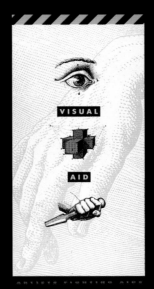

Poster design for Visual
Aid, Artists Fighting
AIDS, San Francisco,
California. Symbols of
the artist (eye, chisel) are
bound by the symbol
of the three-dimensional
cross to bring awareness
of the loss in the art
community. Designers,
Jennifer Morla, Sharrie
Brooks.

Logo design for Biscotti
Nucci, old-world recipe
Italian biscuits pro-
duced by Prodotti Nucci,
Napa, California.
Designer, Jennifer Morla.
▼

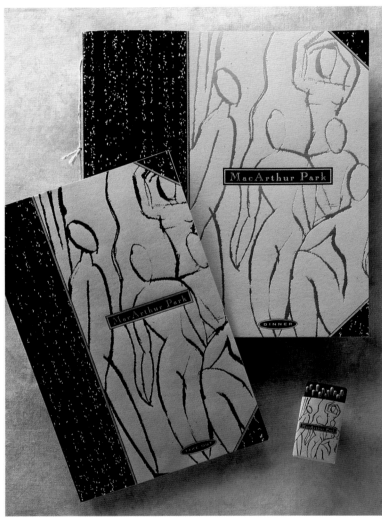

Menu and matchbook
designs for MacArthur
Park restaurant, for
Spectrum Foods, Inc.,
San Francisco, California.
The restaurant is a
popular meeting place
with a creative interior.
The tables are covered
with butcher paper
and crayons are available
to draw on it. Designers,
Jennifer Morla, Jeanette
Aramburu.
▲

Packaging design
for Biscotti Nucci incor-
porates the symbols of
Venice: the winged
lions and the star of
San Marcos. Hand-let-
tering lends an upscale,
authentic quality to the
product. Designers,
Jennifer Morla, Jeanette
Aramburu.
▲

Retail packaging designs for Cocolat, Berkeley, California. The containers were created to facilitate easy dispensing of the product. Package is reusable and makes an attractive gift.
▼

Logo design for LEAP San Francisco's sand-castle contest, an event for children with the participation of local architecture firms. Designer, Jennifer Morla; Illustrator, Jeanette Aramburu.
◄

Levi's Jean Shop and fixture designs for Foote, Cone & Belding, San Francisco, California. The environment enhances the product in a changeable, dynamic space to shop. Designers, Jennifer Morla, Scott Drummond.
▼

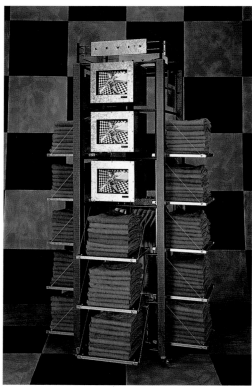

Poster for Levi's Cords, for Levi Strauss & Co., San Francisco, California. The poster gives a tactile sense of the corduroy fabric, while graphically appealing to a 14-24 year-old target audience. Designer and Illustrator, Jennifer Morla; Photographer, Tony Viramontes.
▲

Brochure design for Levi's girls fashions is targeted to a more fashion-forward line for 7-14 year-olds. Designers, Jennifer Morla, Jeanette Aramburu; Photography, Bybee Studios.
▶

This poster (1980) for Levi's 501 Jeans was a radical departure from the full-color western imagery used in prior campaigns. Designer, Jennifer Morla; Photographer, Rick Strauss.

▲

Brochures for Levi's Silver Tab Collection are used to inform store buyers of the styles and garment details of this line. Designer, Jennifer Morla; Illustrators, Jennifer Morla, Erik Watts; Copywriters, Jennifer Morla, Julie Klee; Photographer, Thomas Heinser.

▼

Design for Tuck & Patti's "Dream" album, for Windham Hill Records, Palo Alto, California. Allusions to sleep are evoked by undulating type of song lyrics and surreal blue roses. Designers, Jennifer Morla, Jeanette Aramburu; Photographer, Gerry Bybee/Bybee Studios.

▲

Wells Fargo Bank merchandising campaign effectively simplifies the company's many products and services with a graphic visual link. Historic props reinforce the sense of long-standing quality, and color bars identify specific product groups. Designer, Jennifer Morla; Photographer, Terry Heffernan; Stylist, Holly Stewart.
▼

Wells Fargo Bank VISA/MasterCard. Stagecoach imagery reinforces "oldest bank in the west." Designers, Jennifer Morla, Jeanette Aramburu.
▼

Logo design for Wells Fargo Bank, San Francisco, California. Designer, Jennifer Morla; Calligrapher, Jan Shockner.
►

Calendar design for 1992 American President Lines, Oakland, California. A half-size cover lifts to reveal two globes connected by the APL eagle logo. Each month's photograph depicts goods connected to their destinations. Graphic elements impart a sense of an interconnected, global community. Designers, Jennifer Morla, Sharrie Brooks; Photographer, Henrik Kam; Copywriter, Stefanie Marlis. ▼

Promotion design for Futura typeface, for Mercury Typography, San Francisco, California. The design creates an appreciation of the typeface's history and architectural use. Designer, Jennifer Morla. ◄

Poster design announcing the new site of the San Francisco Museum of Modern Art. Designer, Jennifer Morla. ◄

Paper promotion designs for Simpson Paper Company's Parchment series, "The Art of Writing." Prehistoric and contemporary calligraphy present a condensed timeline of man's tie to the earliest writing surface. Designers, Jennifer Morla, Jeanette Aramburu; Photographer, Michael LaMotte; Stylist, Sara Slavin. ◄

Annual report design for San Francisco International Airport, for the San Francisco Airport Commission. Graphics depict focus between East and West, imports and exports, and tourism. Designer, Jennifer Morla; Illustrator, Guy Billout; Photographer, Tom Tracy; Copywriter, San Fransisco International Airport. ▲

Poster pad designs for Kansas City's Spangler Printers celebrates the company's 50th year in business. Illustrator (Dylan), Richard Mantel.
▼

Muller + Company

4739 Belleview
Kansas City, MO 64112
816/531-1992

Senior management of Muller + Company: (left to right) Mike Alexander, David Marks, John Muller, Kathleen Muller.
▼

One of a series of posters
and ads designed using
animals as analogies
of software products for
Informix Software, Inc.
This particular poster
was so popular that even
the press sheets were
trimmed out to meet
the demand. This was
part of a campaign that
generated over 70,000
leads in six months.
Photographer, David
Ludwigs.
▼

Principals:
John Muller
Kathy Muller
Year Founded: 1983
Size of Firm: 22
Key Clients:
Crown Center
Redevelopment,
The Des Moines Register,
Hallmark Cards, Inc.,
Marion Merrill Dow, Inc.,
North Kansas City
Hospital,
Sprint,
Tivol Jewelers

Muller + Company

The difference is friendliness.

The Smart Word Processor. Smart*ware*
from Innovative Software

Jacket design of Graphic
Design USA: 12, for
the American Institute
of Graphic Arts incor-
porates the facial features
of our four AIGA
Medalists to create a
unique personality.
Photographer, Michael
Regnier.
◄

John Muller can design on a big budget, a
shoestring budget—or in some cases, no budget
at all. The principal of this Kansas City
design firm, along with its president—his wife—
Kathy Muller, looks at having the occasional
no money project as a challenge rather than an
obstacle. "Kansas City doesn't always produce big
dollars," he admits, but this doesn't prevent him
from being creative in a big way. Founded in 1983,
Muller + Company has achieved a national reputation for integrating advertising and design—two
disciplines more in competition than in coalition—
in projects that really get a client's attention. In large
part, an "enriching" three-year position as art director
with Hallmark Cards gave Muller the print and
production background that is used so successfully
in his work. "Before I got into advertising," Muller
says, " and discovered how interesting it could be,
I had the typical designer's view of it. But then I
began to see that mass-media advertising simply provides a larger audience for our work. By providing
design and advertising to our clients, we become a
much more effective partner in their total marketing
efforts." There is a difference in the Muller + Company
approach, to quote one of their ads:"The difference is
friendliness."

Packaging and point of purchase for Smartware, Great Britian's #1 software product.
▼

Wingz software exhibition design, for Informix Software, Inc., Lenexa, Kansas.
▲

Logo and package design promoting new product campaign for CE Software. Muller also handles all national advertising for CE Software.
▲

Muller + Company

Poster designs for the new opening of Mission Mall, Mission, Kansas. Produced within three weeks on an extremely limited budget, these posters "wallpapered" the mall and were soon collector items.
▼

The Sprint Corporate Brochure features abstract photographs of Kansas City Fountains (Kansas City is Sprint's Headquarters) as they symbolize the Sprint Corporate vision. Photographer: Michael Regnier.
▼

"Save the Wails," poster design for the Kansas City Jazz Commission.
▼

"Home Fires Burning,"
poster design for
Hallmark Hall of Fame
television series. Muller
has produced design for
Hall of Fame productions
for over seven years, and
has received international
recognition for these film
promotions.
▼

Series of ads designed to
increase sales for
classified section of *The
Des Moines Register*. This
campaign resulted in a
27% increase in classified
sales for the Register.
Photographers, Michael
Regnier, Nick Vedros.
▼

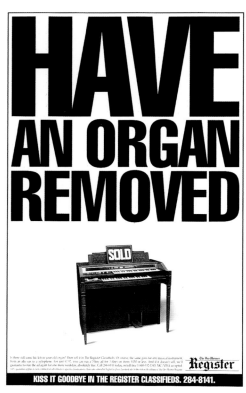

Logo design for
Continuous Quality
Improvement (CQI)
program for client
North Kansas City
Hospital.
▶

"Volume," one of a series
of ads for Tivol Jewelers
which uses store owner
Harold Tivol's words
and portraits. Coupled
with a television and
radio campaign, the store
realized a 40% growth in
new customers in one year.
Photographer, Michael
Regnier.
▼

WE INTRODUCED CHARLIE TO HIS BEST FRIEND.

FINE JEWELRY SPEAKS
FOR ITSELF.
I'M JUST HERE TO
TURN UP THE VOLUME.

HAROLD TIVOL

Tivol Diamonds From $500

TIVOL

220 Nichols Road
The Plaza 531-5800

The Tivol annual Picnic &
Volleyball Blowout

Logo designed for Tivol
Jewelers promoting the
store's annual volleyball
event.
▲

Of course, he was smart enough to look in The Des Moines Register Classifieds, where you can find informative,
entertaining and easy-to-read listings on everything from cars to cattle, from appliances to antiques, from pets to
pianos. Take a look, and you'll see why The Register Classifieds section is Iowa's
biggest shopping center. And to place a classified ad, call 284-8141 or 1-800-532-1585
outside the Des Moines area. **You'll Find A Great Deal In The Register Classifieds.**

The Des Moines Register

Brochure design for the Kansas City Art Institute is used as a fundraising and awareness building tool. Principal photographer, Michael Regnier. ▼

Limuli poster was designed in memory of John Muller's grandfather who owned a produce company. ►

Omni "Call for Entries" designed for the Kansas City Ad Club. Photographers, Nick Vedros, Michael Regnier. ►

Logo design for Cafe Lulu in Kansas City. ▲

"Breaking Through,"
Call for Entries designed
for the Kansas City
Art Directors Club.
Photographers, Hollis
Officer, Nick Vedros.
▼

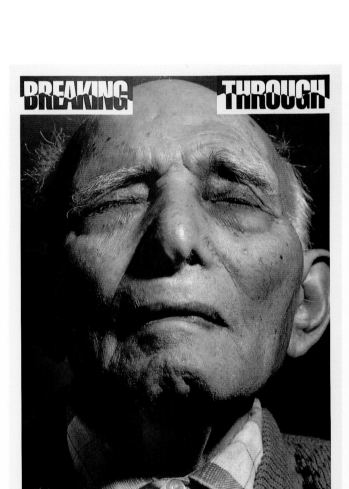

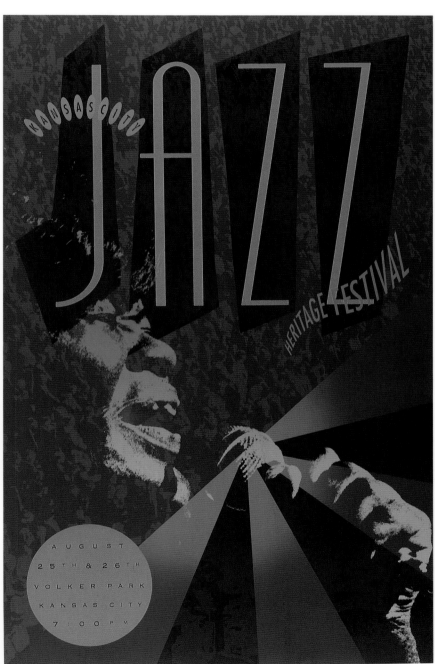

Poster design promoting
annual Jazz Festival,
for the Kansas City Jazz
Commission.
▲

148   **Nesnadny & Schwartz**

10803 Magnolia Drive
Cleveland, OH 44106
216/791-7721

One Bond Street
New York, NY 10012
212/673-8888

Joyce Nesnadny and
Mark Schwartz,
principals of
Nesnadny & Schwartz.
▼

Recruiting brochures for
Ortho Pharmaceutical
Corporation, Raritan,
New Jersey. Creative
Directors, Joyce Nesnadny,
Mark Schwartz; Photo-
graphy, Tony Festa.
▼

Annual report design
for The George Gund
Foundation, Cleveland,
Ohio. Creative Director,
Mark Schwartz; Designer,
Ruth D'Emilia; Photo-
grapher, Michael Book.
▶

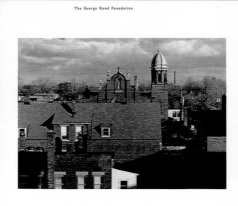

1991 annual report for
University Circle, Inc.
Cleveland, Ohio.
Creative Directors,
Mark Schwartz, Joyce
Nesnadny; Designers,
Joyce Nesnadny,
Jennifer Dye.
▼

Principals:
Joyce Nesnadny
Mark Schwartz
Year Founded: 1981
Size of Firm: 9
Key Clients:
Akron Art Museum,
American Institute
of Architects,
Ameritrust,
Booz, Allen
& Hamilton,
British Petroleum (BP),
Case Western
Reserve University,
Cleveland Institute
of Art,
Eaton Corporation,
Ernst & Young,
Federal Reserve Bank,
George Gund
Foundation,
Invacare,
Richard E.
& David H. Jacobs,
Johnson & Johnson,
Jones, Day Reavis
& Pogue,
Kaiser Permanente,
Ortho Pharmaceutical
Corp.,
Parker Hannifin,
The Progressive
Corporation,
Squire, Sanders &
Dempsey,
TRW,
University Circle, Inc.,
University Hospitals
of Cleveland,
S.D. Warren,
Waxman Industries

Nesnadny & Schwartz

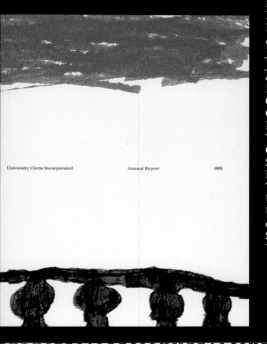

University Circle Incorporated   Annual Report   1991

Walking up the flower ensconced front steps and manicured lawn in the middle of Cleveland's University Circle, you'd think you're coming home rather than going to the design offices of Nesnadny & Schwartz. There is no sign to tell you that behind the homey facade lies fertile design, implemented by a staff for projects that range from graphic identities for a local restaurant, to annual reports for some of the counties largest corporations, to pro bono projects for nonprofit organizations. The partnership of Joyce Nesnadny and Mark Schwartz began when the two were in college. The firm of Nesnadny & Schwartz formally opened their doors for business shortly thereafter. They credit their early success, at least in part, to this absolute lack of "professional" experience. Nesnadny & Schwartz has had the rare opportunity to collaborate with visual artists who normally work within exclusively fine arts venues, bringing art to a different context. "We have never lost our connection to fine art. It continually informs our work as designers." The emphasis is on ideas over style. "If our work has a 'style' it has more to do with the individuals that work here. We are all involved as deeply as possible in our work. We try to give the client the best quality and ideas, while satisfying our own aesthetic needs." Included in all this is an element somewhat off-kilter, but never off center. "Hopefully we don't take ourselves too seriously— the danger most designers fall prey to—there is always room for more humor."

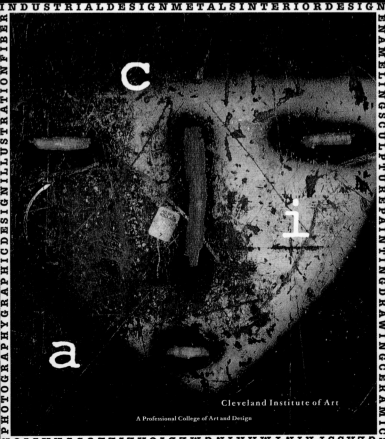

1991-1993 catalog for
the Cleveland Institute
of Art. Designer, Joyce
Nesnadny.
◄

Recruiting publications for the Cleveland Institute of Art. Designers, Joyce Nesnadny, Ruth D'Emilia. ▼

Brochure design for Western Reserve Aids Foundation, Cleveland, Ohio. Designers, Ruth D'Emilia, Okey Nestor. ▶

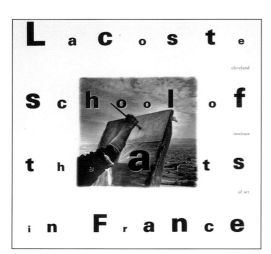

Capabilities brochure for Lacoste School of the Arts, Lacoste, France. Creative Director, Joyce Nesnadny. ▲

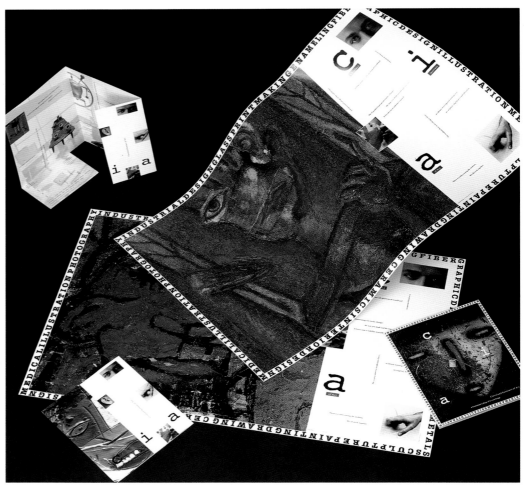

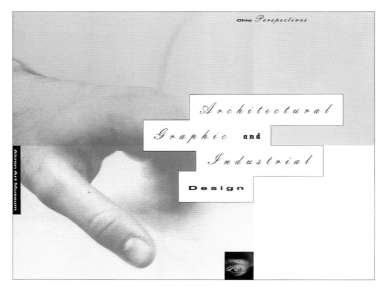

"Ohio Perspectives" exhibition catalog design for Akron Art Museum. Designers, Joyce Nesnadny, Ruth D'Emilia. ◀

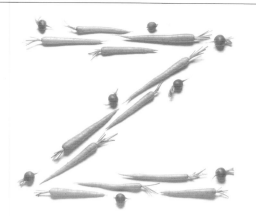

Menu design and graphic
identity system for Z
Contemporary Cuisine.
Creative Directors, Joyce
Nesnadny, Mark Schwartz;
Photographer, Tony Festa.
◀ ▼

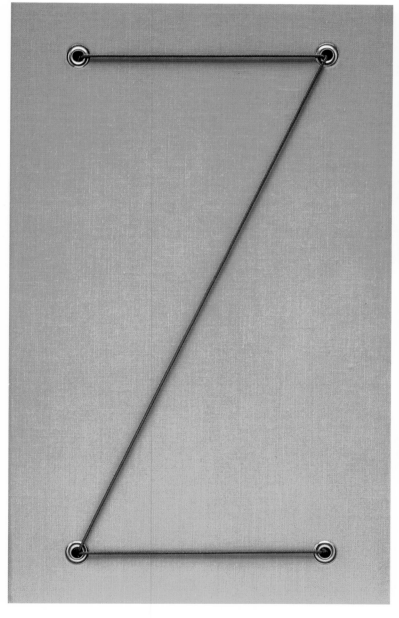

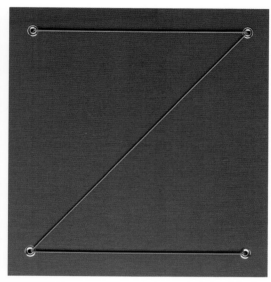

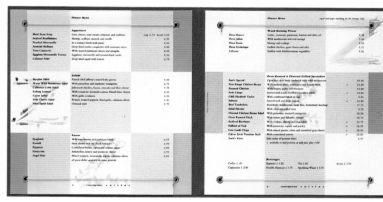

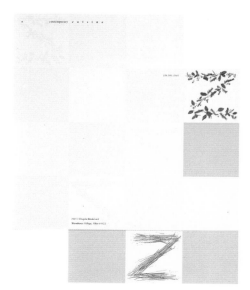

1991 annual report
design for The Progressive
Corporation. Creative
Directors, Joyce Nesnadny,
Mark Schwartz; Artists,
Kay Rosen and Old
Masters.
▼

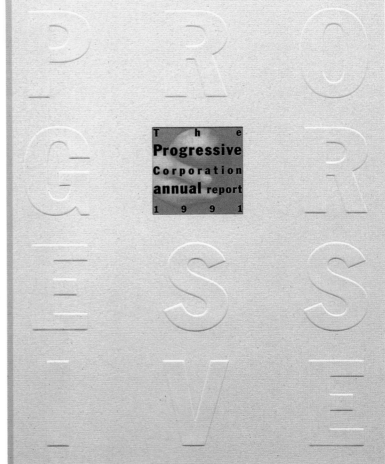

1989 quarterly report
cover designs for The
Progressive Corporation.
Creative Directors,
Joyce Nesnadny, Mark
Schwartz; various artists.
▶

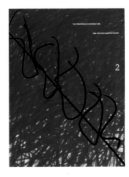

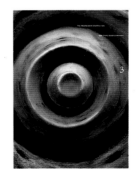

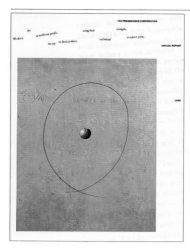
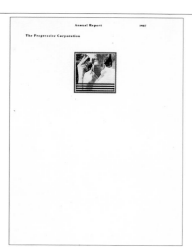

1989,88,87 annual report
cover designs for The
Progressive Corporation.
Creative Directors,
Joyce Nesnadny, Mark
Schwartz; various artists.
◄

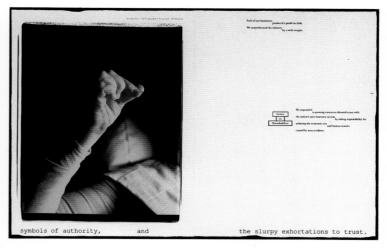

symbols of authority,   and   the slurpy exhortations to trust.

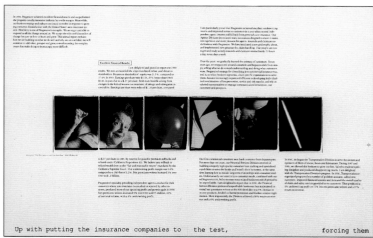

Up with putting the insurance companies to   the test,   forcing them

1990 annual report
design and 1991 quarterly
report design for The
Progressive Corporation.
Creative Directors,
Joyce Nesnadny, Mark
Schwartz; various artists.
▲ ▶

154

National publication design system for Booz, Allen & Hamilton, New York, New York. Includes Graphic Standards Manual and work samples. Creative Directors, Mark Schwartz, Okey Nestor.
▼

Financial services product brochures for The Progressive Corporation. Creative Directors, Joyce Nesnadny, Mark Schwartz; Illustrator, Jo Caress.
▶

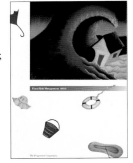

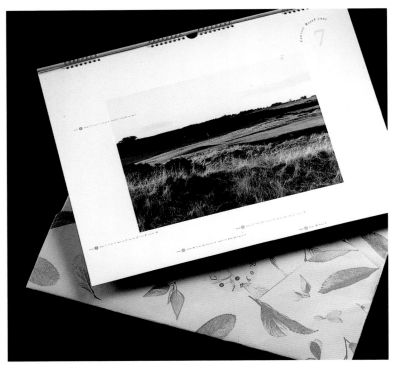

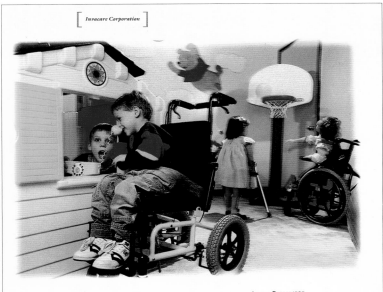

1990 annual report for Invacare Corporation, Cleveland, Ohio. Designers, Joyce Nesnadny, Ruth D'Emilia; Photographers, Jack Van Antwerp, Tony Festa.
▲

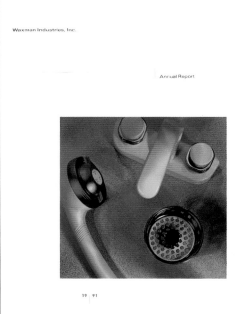

Consort Royal 1990 calendar, paper promotion for Garden City Paper International, Philadelphia, Pennsylvannia. Creative Directors, Joyce Nesnadny, Mark Schwartz; Photographer, Michael Book.
▲

1991 annual report for Waxman Industries, Cleveland, Ohio. Creative Directors, Mark Schwartz, Joyce Nesnadny; Designer, Jennifer Dye.
◀

Society Center real estate marketing package, portfolio and brochures, for Richard E. and David H. Jacobs. Creative Directors Mark Schwartz, Ruth D'Emilia, Okey Nestor; Photographers, Mark Schwartz, Hedrich Blessing. ▼

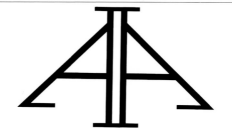

Logo design for the American Institute of Architects. Designer, Okey Nestor. ◄

Building development poster for Ameritrust Center, for Richard E. and David H. Jacobs. Creative Directors, Mark Schwartz, Okey Nestor. ▼

Capabilities brochure design for The Scott Group, Grand Rapids, Michigan. Creative Directors, Joyce Nesnadny, Mark Schwartz; Designers, Joyce Nesnadny, Ruth D'Emilia; Photographers, Mark Schwartz, Craig VanderLende. ►

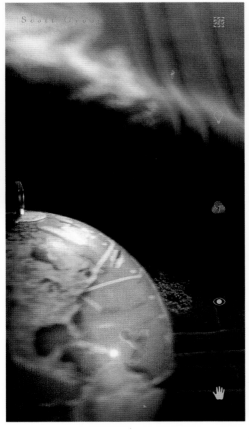

Forrest and Valerie Richardson live and work together in Phoenix, Arizona. They met while working at a national market research firm – they were doing a study about Cheez Whiz. Valerie went on to orchestrate graphics for a local school district. Forrest became the art director at KPHO Television. In 1983 they formed their own firm, Richardson or Richardson. For their clients, Forrest and Valerie have garnered numerous awards and their work has been featured in several leading magazines, exhibitions and textbooks.

Design Travels

Forrest and Valerie Richardson

For a moment, let's set this book aside. Instead, your mission for the next few minutes will be to indulge the following scene. If it makes you feel more comfortable, please feel free to mark your place so you'll know where to return when we've done.

Alright. You're on a lonely stretch of desert highway. It's just after nine o'clock in the morning. You're 150 miles east of the most famous canyon in the world. Already, it's 105 degrees. And, even though you're in what most people think of as America, this really isn't America at all. It's the Navajo Indian Nation and, while there is nothing to see as far as the eye can see, there is at the same time, more than anyone can ever begin to see.

From your perspective, just above the road on the side of a sandstone cliff, you hear only the faintest sounds. Mostly the breeze. Occasionally an insect. But this is all you hear until the next paragraph.

Sensing a distant sound, your head turns quickly to the right. This is a different sound. It isn't the breeze. It isn't an insect. You squint your eyes. This makes it harder to see but apparently increases your ability to hear. Whatever it is, it's coming towards you. It's moving fast. And it's red. Within a few sentences, you guess, it will be right below you.

Just as suddenly as your head turned right, it now turns left. Whatever it was passed by at what you later estimate to have been 80 miles per hour. Because you are observant, you began to recall more clearly what you saw. It was indeed red. Specifically, it was a red Mazda Miata sports car. The top was down and there were two people inside.

The driver was a man. The passenger was a woman. As you think back on the split second it whizzed past, you begin to recall a few details. The woman and the driver had been talking. On her lap, was a Macintosh PowerBook personal computer. Although it was hard to hear above the radio, you overheard a brief portion of their conversation. They were talking about what it meant to be a designer–what kinds of things they felt were important in their professional lives and some of the things they had learned while working together and meeting people. They were writing an essay of sorts. Probably for a design book.

Having noticed some text on the computer screen, you thought back to what you saw. Quickly, you recapped the highlights of what you remembered by writing key words on the palm of your hand. Later, at a small trading post, you expounded on the notes, dictating them to an old Indian woman who typed them on an even older typewriter. They went something like this:

1. Designers need to know 25 things. The first one of these things is not necessarily on this list.

2. All good design requires appreciation for the product, service, or idea the designer is designing for. It's not a good idea to design without background information. It's never a good idea to design without clarity on what is being done by when and by who and for whom and for how much.

3. Usually, clients are people. They should make a better designer out of you. You should make a better client out of them. Saul Bass said this, but probably much better.

4. With few exceptions, good design should generate profit for a minimum of two people; the person needing the design and the person doing the design.

5. Designers give away far too many rights. Try thinking of designs as songs.

6. Good design is usually simple. Simple is very difficult to master.

7. "There is no such thing as a false idea."—U.S. Supreme Court in a 1974 decision written by Justice Lewis F. Powell.

8. Most good ideas usually involve a degree of risk. As Charles Lindbergh put it, "I don't believe in taking foolish chances, but nothing can be accomplished without taking chances at all." Or, Walt Disney's famous observation, "It's kind of fun to do the impossible." Designers are really inventors.

9. Almost all design requires some degree of writing. Copy is not grey, insignificant stuff.

10. A designer must be observant to everything because everything is or influences design.

11. Build things to last. There are few substitutes for quality. Quality is not simply how you produce something physically, it is also how something communicates and functions.

12. Design has no limits. Lou Dorfsman, art director for CBS Television, once arranged for newsman Walter Cronkite to make a guest appearance on the Mary Tyler Moore Show. It not only boosted the ratings of Mary's show, it also raised the ratings of the CBS Evening News. What originally started out as a desperate request for newspaper ads, was instead handled with a few well designed phone calls.

13. A designer must respect natural resources and this is not satisfied by how many times one uses that cute little trilogy of clockwise arrows.

14. A designer must be resourceful. Don't take "no" for an answer unless it's the answer you're looking for.

15. On a big piece of white paper, write "THE WORK" in 300 point type. Under it, write "THE CLIENT" in 120 point type. Under that, write "YOU" in 24 point type. You now understand how important egos are in design. Finished products and results are what count. Wieden & Kennedy uses this to help creative people understand the previous sentence.

16. You will always find out who makes the decisions. It is usually better to do this up front.

17. The kind of work you do is the kind of work you get.

18. Design is a universal language. Don't confine yourself when there is so much to see and so much to share.

19. Always support good design. Buy it. Recommend it. Promote it.

20. Always support the fields of architecture, interior design, and industrial design. Perhaps they will support you. If not, you still have the option of criticizing the typefaces they choose.

21. Students are much more than pesky sources of resumes and portfolios. They are also pesky sources of ideas—the ideas your clients will be looking for tomorrow.

22. Hire people who are better than yourself. End relationships that go nowhere. Never burn bridges; you never know when you might need to cross back over them.

23. A designer should be happy. Work hard and play hard. As John Lennon put it, "Life is what happens to you while you're making other plans." You cannot design things for people unless you experience the condition of being a person yourself every so often.

24. "Wait too long for your ship to come in, and your pier may collapse."—Morey Amsterdam said this to "Sally" in one of his great moments on the Dick Van Dyke Show. A designer needs to take responsibility. This is not a dress rehearsal.

25. Finally, of all the reasons and all the inspirations to live a life in design, the single greatest attraction is in never knowing what you will learn and experience and create next.

Peterson & Company

2200 North Lamar Street
Suite 310
Dallas, TX 75202
214/954-0522

Promotion brochure design for Mead Moistrite Matte paper, for Mead Fine Paper Division, Dayton, Ohio. Designer, Bryan L. Peterson; Photographer, Tom Ryan.
▼

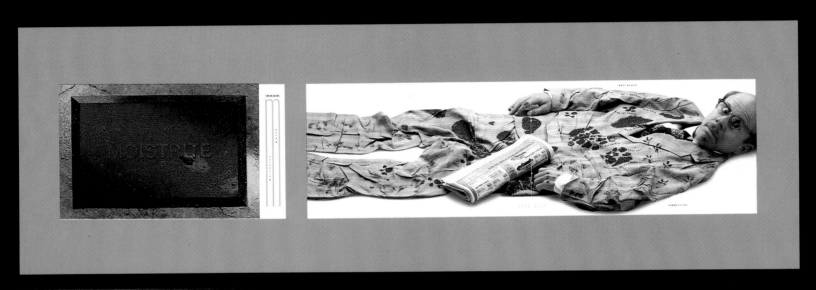

Directory design for the American Society of Magazine Photographers, Dallas, Texas. Designer, Scott Paramski.
▲

Left to right, front row: Scott Ray, Bryan Peterson; back row, Nhan Pham, Jan Wilson, Sharon Gorham, Scott Paramski, and Karla Campalans of Peterson & Company. Photographer; Robb Debenport
▶

Principal:
Bryan L. Peterson
Year Founded: 1985
Size of Firm: 7
Key Clients:
Baker & Botts,
Centex Corporation,
Central & Southwest
Services,
Columbia University,
Cybertek Corporation,
EDS,
Federal Reserve Bank,
Frito-Lay, Inc.,
GTE,
Maxus Energy
Corporation,
Mead Paper,
Mothers Against Drunk
Driving (MADD),
Northern Telecom,
PepsiCo, Inc.,
Southern Methodist
University,
Uniden Satellite
Television

Peterson & Company

Poster design for the
Fourth Annual Highland
Village Balloon Festival,
Dallas, Texas. Designer
and Illustrator, Bryan L.
Peterson.
▼

Peterson & Company has been referred to as a firm that doesn't promote a particular style. Formed in 1985, Bryan Peterson built his company with the determination to hire good designers and then trust them to design. Peterson has no desire to be pigeon-holed into a design style and, in fact, believes the concept of the design will provide clues to the appropriate style of execution. Each of the five designers at Peterson & Company not only has the freedom to design, but is encouraged to experiment with different looks and also service a particular group of clients. Bryan Peterson himself is insistent on remaining a designer rather than overseer. He not only directs his own projects, he also designs and produces them on the computer. Peterson is also recognized nationally as an illustrator and, along with the other designers on staff, illustrates many of the projects for Peterson & Company.

Vigon Seireeni poster
design, for the
Dallas Society of Visual
Communication,
Dallas, Texas.
Designer, Scott Ray.
▶

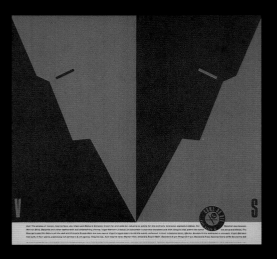

Peterson & Company

Annual report for
Lifetime Products,
Dallas, Texas.
Designer, Scott
Paramski;
Photographers, Tom
Ryan, Gerry Kano.
▶

Annual report, 1989,
for Mothers Against
Drunk Driving
(MADD), Irving, Texas.
Designer, Bryan L.
Peterson; Photographer,
Tom Ryan.
▲

Annual report, 1990, for
Centex Corporation,
Dallas, Texas. Designer,
Bryan L. Peterson;
Photographers, Robb
Debenport, Gerry Kano.
▶

Logo design for
Children's Presbyterian
Healthcare Center,
Dallas, Texas. Designer,
Scott Paramski.
▲

Annual report, 1990,
for Maxus Energy
Corporation, Dallas,
Texas. Designer, Scott
Ray; Photographers,
Robb Debenport,
Gerry Kano.
▼

CYBERTEK

Annual
Report
Nineteen
Ninety
One

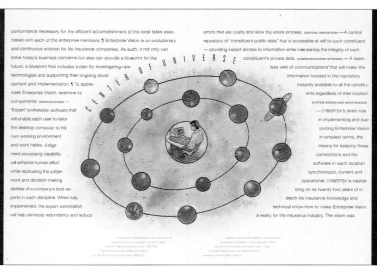

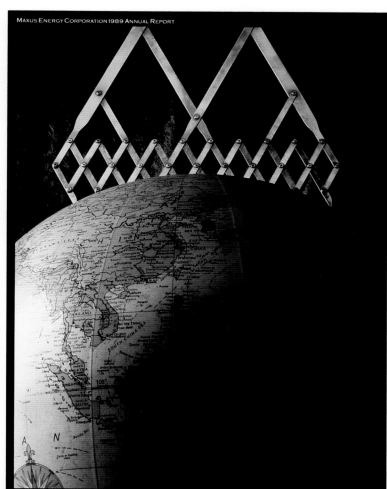

MAXUS ENERGY CORPORATION 1989 ANNUAL REPORT

Annual report, 1991, for
Cybertek Corporation,
Dallas, Texas. Designer,
Scott Ray; Illustrator,
Greg King; Photographer,
Peter Lacker.
◀

Bandwagon Magazine design for Frito-Lay, Inc., Plano, Texas. Designers, Scott Ray, Jan Wilson; Photographer, Peter Lacker. ▼

Shopping bag design for Aldus Corporation, Seattle, Washington. The bag was designed and illustrated on the computer to highlight the qualities of an Aldus freehand software program. Designer and Illustrator, Jan Wilson. ◄

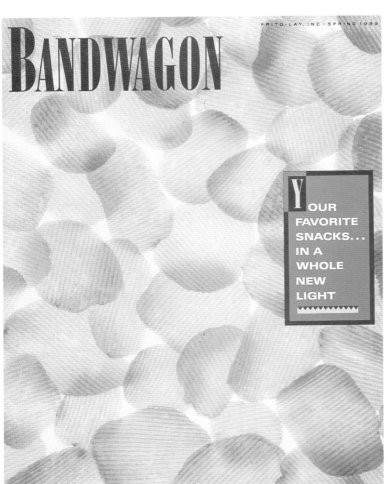

Brochure design for GTE, Dallas, Texas. Designer, Scott Paramski; Photographer, Robert Latorre. ▶

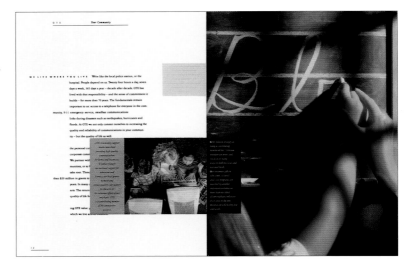

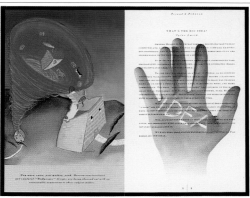

Promotional brochure
for Friend & Johnson
artists reps, Dallas,
Texas. Art Director
and Designer,
Bryan L. Peterson.
◀

SOUL OF A SYBARY

A JAPANESE CAR COMPANY SHIFTS ITS VOICE

The building is a blocky, bold monolith of angles, edges and rectangles. If the soul of an automobile has colors, they're all here, on the exterior and throughout the carpets, walls and fixtures of the new office complex. Slate gray like cast aluminum. A charcoal hue befitting an engine block. Black as flat as anodized body trim. The gleaming mirror-metal of chrome. Glassy expanses like great windshields. ○ Inside, an atrium pierces the heart of the modern seven-story building—a huge, cylindrical elevator tower tying the levels together. As you peer up from the lobby, it makes the office complex look eerily as though it's a luxurious gantry for a rocket awaiting

AND DATA SYSTEM INTO FOUR-WHEEL DRIVE.

countdown. ○ Actually it's the new headquarters of Subaru of America, in Cherry Hill, New Jersey. Subaru is the U.S. importer of some unusual Japanese cars—a company that has carved out a tidy niche for itself in a crowded automotive market by dealing in distinctive small cars that some still think "odd and somewhat quirky," in the words of Subaru Director of Public Relations Fred Heiler. ○ Others, however, increasingly regard Subaru as the progenitor of one of the hotter new automotive markets: on-road passenger cars with four-wheel drive (4WD). Off-road four-wheeling has been around for decades—Jeeps, fat-tired pickups and the like—but only in the last half-dozen years has everybody from Porsche to Ford begun offering the option of powering all four corners of pure highway machinery.

6

7

Logo design for
American Federal Bank,
Dallas, Texas. Designer,
Bryan L. Peterson.
◀

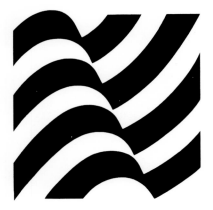

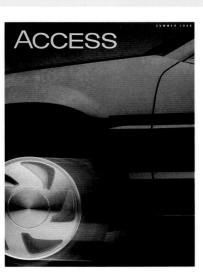

ACCESS

"Soul of a Suburu" spread
and cover for Access
Magazine, Northern
Telecom, Dallas, Texas.
Designer, Bryan L.
Peterson; Photographer,
Tom Ryan.
◀

Promotion design
for Bucknell University,
Lewisburg, Pennsylvania.
Designers, Bryan L.
Peterson, Scott Paramski;
Photographer, Paul
Talley.
▼

Annual report, 1990,
for the Dallas Zoological
Society, Dallas, Texas.
Designer, Scott Ray;
Illustrator, Bryan L.
Peterson.
▶

Peterson & Company

Design of SMU Magazine, for Southern Methodist University, Dallas, Texas. Designers, Jan Wilson, Nhan T. Pham; Photographer, Paul Talley.
▼

Logo design for the Dallas Repertory Theatre, Dallas, Texas. Designer, Scott Ray.
◄

Brochure design for the Dallas Repertory Theatre, Dallas, Texas. Designer, Scott Ray.
▼

Brochure design for Young Audiences of Greater Dallas, Dallas, Texas. Designer, Scott Ray; Illustrator, Bryan L. Peterson.
◄

Barron Hilton Soaring Cup poster, for Hilton Hotels, Beverly Hills, California. The world-wide event pits European and American pilots against each other in a year-long sailplane competition. The poster is part of an overall program that includes booklets, exhibits and commemorative items. Designers, Forrest Richardson, Valerie Richardson; Photographer, Kevin Cruff.

▼

Richardson or Richardson

The Old Hess Farmhouse
1301 East Bethany
Home Road
Phoenix, AZ 85014
602/266-1301

Pacific Associate Office
Central Ochanomizu
Building
2-13-4, Janda-awajicho,
Chiyoda-ku, Tokyo 101,
Japan

Europe Associate Office
The Maltings, Wilson
Close, Stevengate,
Hertford, SG1 4TD
England

Forrest and Valerie
Richardson, principals
of Richardson or
Richardson.

▼

Trademark/symbol of Arrowhead regional shopping center, for Westcor Developers, Phoenix, Arizona. Designer, Debi Young-Mees.

▲

Tradeshow exhibit for DigiType, Phoenix, Arizona, a company which specializes in digital type fonts. The interactive installation allows prospective clients to have a Polaroid snapshot taken with a favorite letter. Designer, Forrest Richardson; Space Planner, Valerie Richardson.

◄

"Jinglebellshammer" for Rowland Companies General Contractors, Arizona, California and Wisconsin. Each year a new tool is selected as the focus of a direct mail promotion. Creative Director, Forrest Richardson.
▼

Principals:
Forrest Richardson
Valerie Richardson
Year Founded: 1983
Size of Firm: 8
Key Clients:
Access Laserpress,
Apple Computer, Inc.,
City of Phoenix,
Communication Arts Magazine,
Cowles Media,
Darcy Paper Company,
Del Webb Corporation,
Disney,
Fiesta Canning Company,
Gilbert Paper Co.,
Golf Management International,

Hilton Hotels,
Hopper Paper/Georgia Pacific,
Jackrabbit Spice Co.,
Macayo Mexican Restaurants,
Mitsui/USA,
PC Globe, Inc.,
The Phoenix Zoo,
Rowland Contructors,
Software Marketing Corporation,
Westcor Developers,
Wilderness Products

Richardson or Richardson

THE JINGLEBELLSHAMMER

This little known artifact originated in Northern Europe centuries ago. It was used by carpenters working through the holiday season as a sign of cheer and goodwill.

Rowland Constructors revives this tradition with resounding wishes for a cheerful holiday and a new year that rings with excitement.

Stationery design for J.W. Tumbles chain of children's gymnasiums based in San Diego, California. The colored symbols are printed in quantity on self-adhesive labels and then randomly attached to the one-color stationery. Designers, Forrest Richardson, Valerie Richardson.
▲

Aluminum and steel chess set. Designer, Forrest Richardson.
▶

Richardson or Richardson may best be described as a group of designers who write and writers who design. While many design firms purposefully shy away from advertising and attention to the written word, Richardson or Richardson has integrated the very essence of persuasion into the process of conceptual thinking. Design, in their work, goes far beyond decoration. Ideas are paramount and require thinking beyond color and texture, and far beyond style. Established in 1983, the firm has built a national reputation and client base while holding onto their original commitment to taking risks with thought-provoking work. Partners in work and marriage as well, Forrest and Valerie Richardson prefer working towards a "big picture," on encompassing work rather than project work. Their work has crossed several boundaries, from retail and entertainment to corporate and institutional. They have also built a strong reputation in two other areas of specialty. First, in the golf industry as experienced consultants who understand the game's nuances and can approach marketing and signage projects with ease. Second, through Ecodea, a division of Richardson or Richardson which provides diverse environmental design services from packaging to completely "re-thinking" a project in environmental terms. This diversity underscores an enthusiasm for the unexpected and unexplored. As Valerie Richardson attests, "There's nothing more exciting and challenging than doing something which hasn't been done before. This is why we're in business."

Disney's Bonnet Creek Golf Club entry sculpture, emblem designs and signage elements for Disney Development Company, Orlando, Florida. The comprehensive program encompassed print graphics, merchandise and environmental design. Designers, Forrest Richardson, Debi Young-Mees, Neill Fox; Landscape Architect, Sharon Fowler. ▼

Trademark for Wilderness Products, a manufacturer of backpacks and outdoor equipment, Phoenix, Arizona. Designer, Forrest Richardson. ◄

A retail catalog and consumer magazine ad for the Takara Bicycles division of Mitsui/USA. Designers, Forrest Richardson, Valerie Richardson; Writer, Forrest Richardson; Photographer, Craig Wells. ▲ ►

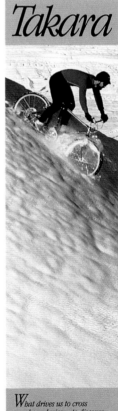

Takara

What drives us to cross new boundaries — to discover new horizons? We believe it is the very same ingenuity that has made us a leader in creating new bicycles. Discover Takara. Discover what's next.

For your nearest dealer call 1-800-4-TAKARA. In Oklahoma call 404-232-4922.

Packaging design
and menu, for T.C.
Eggington's Restaurant,
Mesa, Arizona. Designers,
Forrest Richardson,
Valerie Richardson;
Illustrator, Ken Jacobsen;
Writer, Forrest Richardson.
▼

**Richardson
or Richardson**

Trademark for La Vue
Restaurant, San Diego,
California. Designers,
Forrest Richardson,
Valerie Richardson.
▶

Poster design for the
Phoenix Marathon.
Designer, Forrest
Richardson.
▼

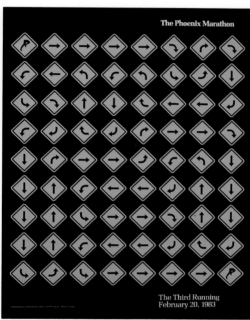

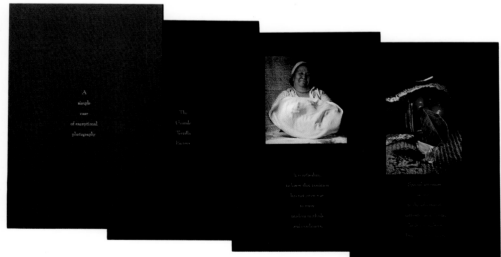

The Grande Tortilla
Factory book for The
Gayle Studio, Phoenix,
Arizona. Designers,
Forrest Richardson,
Debi Young-Mees;
Photographer, Rick
Gayle.
▲

"Blocks" television spot for Sunrise Preschools, part of a corporate image campaign that includes radio, outdoor and print advertisements. Sunrise operates schools in several states. Art Directors, Forrest Richardson, Valerie Richardson; Writer, Forrest Richardson; Director, Brad Sykes.
▼

**Richardson
or Richardson**

Corporate identity design and direct marketing for Sunrise Preschools. New schools are introduced via die-cut cardboard "door hangers" delivered in the school's neighborhood. The tiered program begins with a shovel announcing "ground breaking" and concludes with a key indicating the "doors are now open".

Construction site signs reinforce the campaign. Designers, Forrest Richardson, Valerie Richardson; Writers, Forrest Richardson, Valerie Richardson.
▼

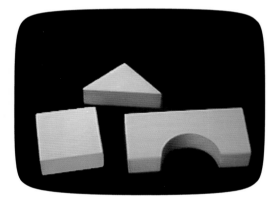

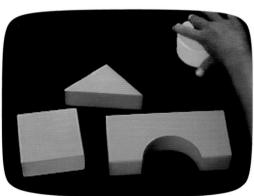

Sunrise.
The right preschool.

In the Works newsletter design for Summa Associates, Tempe, Arizona. Designer, Valerie Richardson.
▲

"Extra Neat Stuff" van design for Sunrise Preschools. The van is part of a separate program offering after school activities such as gymnastics, ballet and swimming. Designer, Valerie Richardson; Illustrator, Rick Kirkman.
▼

Trademark design for Details Event Planning Group, Phoenix, Arizona. Creative Director, Forrest Richardson.
▶

Details

Catalog for Howard's Simple Wooden Toy Company, Pomfret Center, Connecticut. The design uses materials and bindings similar to children's books. Designer, Valerie Richardson; Writer, Forrest Richardson; Photographer, Craig Wells.
▼

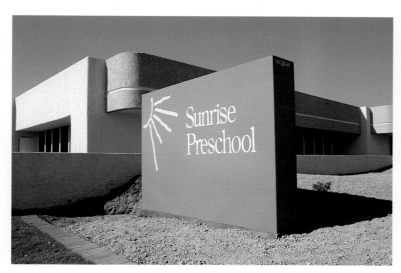

We're building another Sunrise Preschool. Call 878-6556

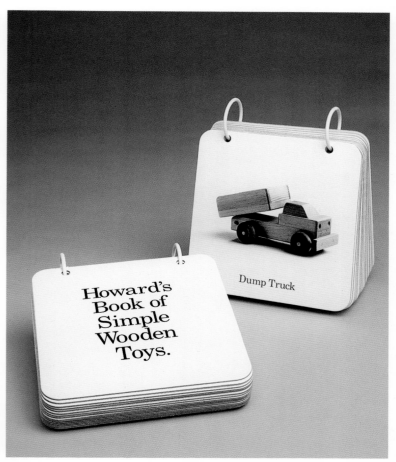

Dump Truck

Howard's Book of Simple Wooden Toys.

Quick Template software packaging design for Software Marketing Corporation, Phoenix, Arizona. Designer, Forrest Richardson; Photographer, Alexander Stricker.
▶

Sunrise Preschools Extra Neat Stuff.

Annual report design for Phoenix Fire Department/Fire-PAL. Designer and Writer, Forrest Richardson; Photographer, Bill Timmerman.
▼

"Globeheads" magazine ad campaign for PC Globe, Inc., Tempe, Arizona. PC Globe makes geography-based software for education, business and travel. Art Director, Debi Young-Mees; Writer, Forrest Richardson; Photographer, Rick Gayle.
▼

Promotional items and packaging design for PC Globe, Inc. The design utilizes traditional maps to communicate the product's similarity to using paper maps and atlases. Cartons are reusable as in-store displays. Creative Director, Forrest Richardson; Designers, Debi Young-Mees, Neill Fox.
▼

Corporate image and marketing materials for Access Laserpress, Phoenix, Arizona. The boomerang icon establishes the essence of the firm's benefit, "Where printing comes back easier." Creative Director, Valerie Richardson; Designer, Debi Young-Mees; Illustrator, Gary Pierazzi.
▼

Richardson or Richardson

Trademark/symbol for Enex Corporation, Prescott, Arizona. The client provides technical machining for aerospace and transportation. Designer, Neill Fox.
►

"Greeting card" photo cubes can be arranged in an endless combination of holiday messages. Designer and Writer, Valerie Richardson; Photographer, Craig Wells.
▼

Photography credits: Bill Timmerman, Rick Gayle, Rusty Flynn and Rodney Rascona.

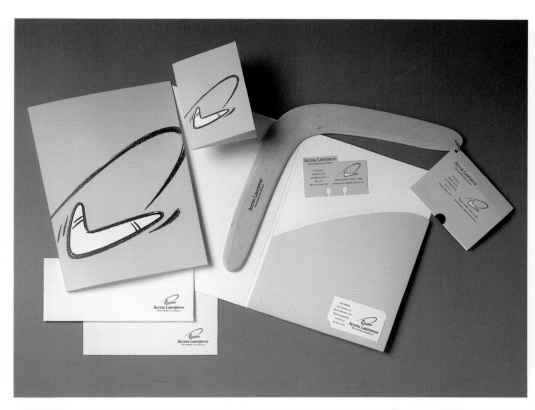

Booklet series promotion for Hopper Paper Company/Georgia Pacific, Atlanta, Georgia. Designers, Valerie Richardson, Debi Young-Mees; Writer, Forrest Richardson; Illustrators, Bob Peters, Neill Fox.
◄

1990 New Year's poster for Siegel Photographic, Phoenix, Arizona. The poster was produced with perforations allowing it to be divided into 1990 individual squares. Designers, Forrest Richardson, Valerie Richardson, and Neill Fox; Writer, Neill Fox.
▲

Schmeltz + Warren

74 Sheffield Road
Columbus, OH 43214
614/262-3055

Catherine Schmeltz and
Crit Warren, Principals
of Schmeltz + Warren.
▼

Selection of Ohio images
from Schmeltz + Warren
stock photography. The
in-house collection of
over 2000 photographs
provide visual reference
and creative stimulation.
Photographer,
Crit Warren.
▼

Ohio Media Equipment
Access poster, for
the Ohio Arts Council,
Columbus, Ohio.
Utilizing a frame-grab-
ber board in a Mac,
images of various rental
equipment were blended
into a video micro/macro
map of Ohio. Designer
and Photographer,
Crit Warren.
◄

Mailing stickers for the
Columbus Society of
Communicating Arts
(CSCA), Columbus, Ohio.
The stickers were used
on the organization's
monthly newsletter
"Mechanism." Designer
and Photographer,
Crit Warren.
▲

Principals:
Crit Warren
Catherine Schmeltz
Year Founded: 1980
Size of Firm: 2
Key Clients:
ABB Asea
Brown Boveri,
CompuServe,
Macmillan Publishing,
OCLC Online Computer
Library Center, Inc.,
Ohio Arts Council,
Ohio College
Association,
Tidewater
Health Care,
Wendy's
International, Inc.

Schmeltz + Warren

Cover photo illustrations
of *Theory Into Practice*,
a journal of The Ohio
State University
College of Education,
Columbus, Ohio.
The illustrations capture
the essence of the
journal's complex con-
tents. Designer and
Photographer,
Crit Warren.
◄

W e think first, then design," is the creative principle behind the success of Schmeltz + Warren. As Crit Warren explains, "We start with concepts, not deco- rative layouts. We want an idea, not some graphic mannerism, to drive the solution." And they like to push those ideas, seeking to create a tension in the viewer. According to Catherine Schmeltz, "We like it when our work is praised, but in certain ways we're happy when it's received less favorably. We want to elicit stronger emotions than just passive acceptance." Much of their work is complex, with heavily layered information, type merging into image and image into type, in ways only recently made possible by the computer. "Type is water now; pictures are too," says Warren. The results are simultaneously experimental and complex, yet strike a balance between readability and legibility, graphic impact and simple clarity. By rejecting the obvious and satisfying their own aes- thetics, Schmeltz + Warren do indeed take risks, but ones that are likely to be approved because clients have shared in the process. "We don't 'get away' with anything. Our clients are always in on our projects. They're more likely to approve risky work if they know how it got that way."

New Marketing
Concepts and
Technologies brochure,
for The Advertising
Federation
of Columbus and
Business First,
Columbus, Ohio. 35mm
photographs of found
scrap metal were scanned
into a Mac and color
enhanced. They acted as
metaphors to the
seminars' different
agendas. Designer and
Photographer,
Crit Warren.
▶

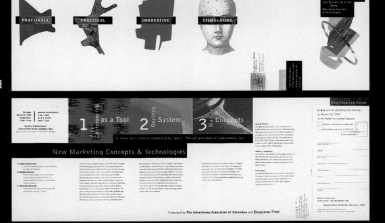

Schmeltz + Warren

Spreads from '91/'92 and '92/'93 editions of "Toward College In Ohio," an informational guide and sourcebook designed each year for The Ohio College Association, Columbus, Ohio. Aimed at 16- to 18-year olds, and not parents or guidance counselors, the brochures present basic information in a format that holds the prospective student's attention. Designer and Photographer, Crit Warren; Editor, Katherine Williams Wright. ▼ ►

in oHIo

tɘɛ ɒɘƨ ƨɘt

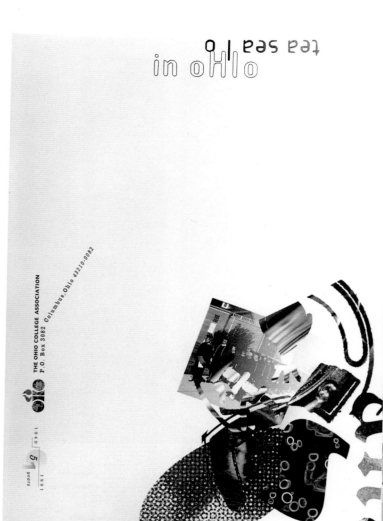

THE OHIO COLLEGE ASSOCIATION
P.O. Box 3082 Columbus Ohio 43210-0082

TOWARD CoLLEgE in OhiO

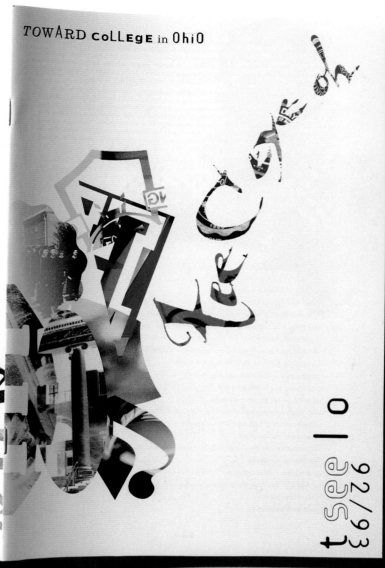

92/93

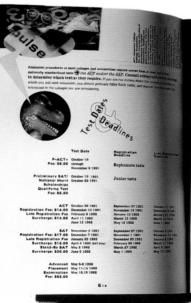

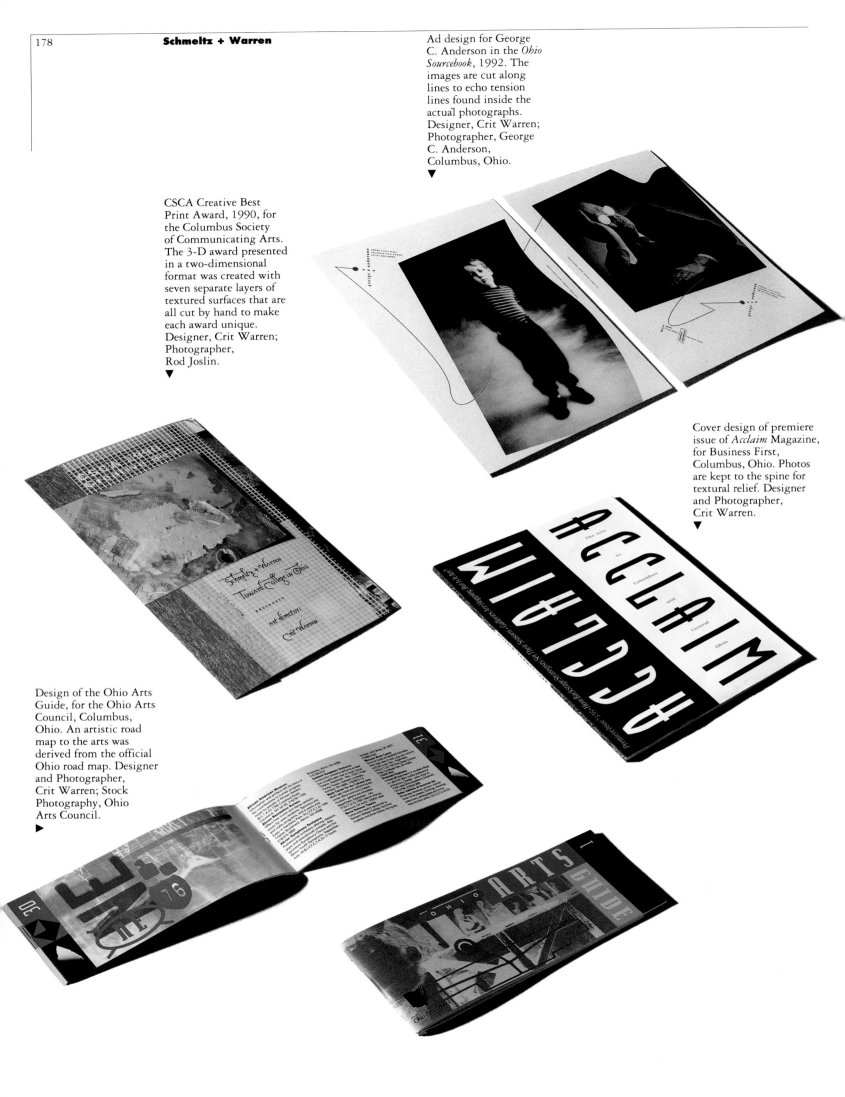

Ad design for George
C. Anderson in the *Ohio
Sourcebook*, 1992. The
images are cut along
lines to echo tension
lines found inside the
actual photographs.
Designer, Crit Warren;
Photographer, George
C. Anderson,
Columbus, Ohio.
▼

CSCA Creative Best
Print Award, 1990, for
the Columbus Society
of Communicating Arts.
The 3-D award presented
in a two-dimensional
format was created with
seven separate layers of
textured surfaces that are
all cut by hand to make
each award unique.
Designer, Crit Warren;
Photographer,
Rod Joslin.
▼

Cover design of premiere
issue of *Acclaim* Magazine,
for Business First,
Columbus, Ohio. Photos
are kept to the spine for
textural relief. Designer
and Photographer,
Crit Warren.
▼

Design of the Ohio Arts
Guide, for the Ohio Arts
Council, Columbus,
Ohio. An artistic road
map to the arts was
derived from the official
Ohio road map. Designer
and Photographer,
Crit Warren; Stock
Photography, Ohio
Arts Council.
▶

Ad design for George C. Anderson in the *Ohio Sourcebook*, 1991. The photographer's working personality is conveyed through the specific type words added on to each image. Designer, Crit Warren; Photographer, George C. Anderson.
▼

Guide to Ohio Media Equipment Access Sites, a brochure designed for the Ohio Arts Council. Information for the media access site is differentiated by typography. Designer and Photographer, Crit Warren.
▼

Call For Entries, 1990, for the Columbus Society of Communicating Arts. Produced inexpensively, computer laserwriter print-outs were used for the final art. Designer and Photographer, Crit Warren.
▼

Poster entry for the Christopher Columbus Quincentennial Jubilee Commission, Columbus, Ohio. Images from four photographers were scanned and composed to layout, then made into a single 8x10 transparency. Designer, Crit Warren; Photographers, Larry Hamill, D.R. Goff, Ted Rice, George C. Anderson; Electronic Production, Chris Graham (Chroma Studios).
▼

Dewey Decimal Classification poster design, for OCLC Online Computer Library Center, Inc., Dublin, Ohio. 100 classifications are listed in an accessible format that blends historical imagery with modern technology. Designer, Crit Warren.
▼

"The Illustrators' Tale," spread from May 1992 issue of "Mechanism," for the Columbus Society of Communicating Arts. Two local illustrators are represented with both visual and verbal information. Designer and Photographer, Crit Warren; Copywriters, Dave Mankins, Michael Linley.
▶

Photo illustrations for the Tenth Anniversary invitation for re:Source Marketing, Inc., Columbus, Ohio. The images all incorporate visual puns of party words. Designer, Crit Warren.
◀

Creative Best Show Catalog, 1990, for the Columbus Society of Communicating Arts. Printers make-ready sheets were run on cover stock, with text carried on plastic overlays that created random patterns on each cover. Designer, Crit Warren; Copywriters, Catherine Schmeltz, Doug Burdick; Photographers, George C. Anderson and Tom Dubanowich (winning entries), Ted Rice (judges), Crit Warren (editorial).
▼

Membership recruitment circular, 1990, for the Columbus Society of Communicating Arts. Directed to the graphic arts membership, the brochure literally reflects the reader beside the line, "Membership improves self-image." Designer and Photographer, Crit Warren; Copywriter, Tom Bedway.
▶

182 **Sibley / Peteet Design, Inc.**

965 Slocum
Dallas, TX 75207
214/761-9400

Don Sibley and Rex
Peteet, Principals of
Sibley/Peteet Design, Inc.
▼

Logo design for
Shavano Park / Melvin
Simon, Indianapolis.
Designer and Illustrator,
Rex Peteet.
▼

FASHION ISLAND
NEWPORT BEACH CALIFORNIA

Fashion Island Re-
Grand Opening-poster
design for Fashion Island
Center, Newport Beach,
California. Designer and
Illustrator, Don Sibley.
▲

Poster design announc-
ing speaker Martin
Pedersen on the theme,
"The purchase and
redesign of *Graphis*
and its various publica-
tions," for the Dallas
Society of Visual
Communications,
Dallas. Designer,
Illustrator, and Copy-
writer, Rex Peteet.
▶

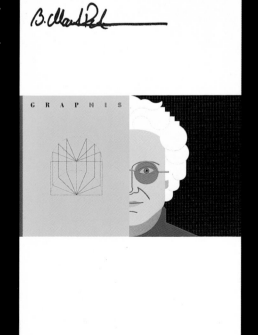

Logo design for
AeroCorp, Lake City,
Florida. Designer,
Rex Peteet; Design
Consultant, Mantz &
Associates Design
Group, Dallas.
▲

Sibley/Peteet Design, Inc.

Principles:
Don Sibley
Rex Peteet
Year Founded: 1982
Size of Firm: 10
Key Clients:
Ameritrust,
American Heart
Association,
Dallas Museum of Art,
Donahue Schriber,
Fashion Island Center,
Georgetown Park,
GSD&M,
Houghton Mifflin,
James River Corporation,
JMB Realty,
LaSalle Partners,
Marcel Schurman,
Mary Kay Cosmetics,
Memorex,
Milton Bradley Co.,
Morris & Fellows,
Novikoff, Inc.,
Treacy Marketing
Group,
Today's Kids,
Weyerhaeuser Paper
Company

Chili Cookoff poster for
Designers of Dallas.
Designer, Illustrator and
Copywriter, Don Sibley.
▲

Logo design for Lone
Star Donuts, a Texas
pastry baker, Dallas.
Designer, Rex Peteet;
Agency, Saunders,
Lubinsky & White,
Dallas.
▶

Partners Rex Peteet and Don Sibley met
in the piney woods of East Texas 20 years
ago. Fate and a terrific design climate
led them both to Dallas, where they honed
their craft at such firms as the Richards
Group and Pirtle Design. A decade ago Sibley/Peteet
Design, Inc. was born, where they have meshed their
illustrative graphic styles in work for toy companies,
cosmetics manufacturers, fashion, real estate and entertainment industries. Peteet's and Sibley's writing
skills have led naturally to distinctive, engaging problem solving with solid concepts and words first—
and beautiful design second. For design that is fun
and games, they admit, "We enjoy and pursue companies and industries that allow us to create for young
audiences, where our colorful graphic styles can be
used to their fullest." This is borne out in any number
of their packaging designs for Milton Bradley or Today's
Kids, among others; however, they bring a youthful
approach to more formal client projects as well. "We
are re-marketers. We often are commissioned to
freshen up corporate images through identity, advertising and collateral programs."

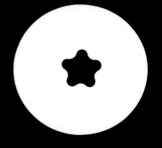

Sibley/Peteet Design, Inc.

Prism pocket folder and product brochure, for Ameritrust, Cleveland. The sales presentation materials introduce a new, high-tech employee benefit 401 (k) plan. Designer, Don Sibley; Illustrator, Mick Wiggins, Berkeley, California; Copywriter, John Eikmeyer, Dallas.
▼

Logo design for Patricia Silverman, design consultant. Designer, John Evans.
◄

Game packaging designs for Milton Bradley, East Longmeadow, Massachusetts. Designers and Illustrators, Don Sibley, Rex Peteet, John Evans, Diana McKnight, David Beck; Additional illustration, Gary Baseman.
▲

Acapella, Genji, and Angelfire limited edition holiday fragrance packaging for Mary Kay Cosmetics, Dallas. Designer, Don Sibley.
▲

"Portrait" promotion for James River Corporation, Southampton, Pennsylvania. This book is a complete specifying guide and chip chart, including all premium grades. Designer, Rex Peteet; Copywriters, Mary Langridge and Rex Peteet; Photographers, Bobby Badger and Elle Schuster; Illustrators Rex Peteet and Bryan Leister. ▼

Shopping bag design for Collin Creek Mall, JMB, Chicago. The bag serves as a walking billboard for the client. Designer and Copywriter, Rex Peteet; Illustrator, Anthony Russo. ◄

Logo design for Image Express printers, Dallas. Designer, Judy Dolim. ►

"Cat-A-Log" promotional brochure for Weyerhaeuser Paper Company, Valley Forge, Pennsylvania. Designer, Don Sibley; Copywriter, John Frazier; Various Photographers and Illustrators. ▼

"Details on Flannel" paper promotion campaign for James River Corporation, Southampton, Pennsylvania. Designer, Rex Peteet; Copywriter, Lee Herrick and Rex Peteet; Illustration, Sibley/Peteet Design, Inc.; Photographer, Gary McCoy. ◄

"Jaguar" promotional brochure introduces the new line of premium uncoated text and cover papers, for Weyerhaeuser Paper Company, Valley Forge, Pennsylvania. Designer, Don Sibley; Copywriter, John Frazier; Various Photographers and Illustrators. ▲

Sibley/Peteet Design, Inc.

Corporate identity for GSD&M, Austin. The agency consists of four principals with different talents and functions, each is represented with their own distinct initial. Designers, Rex Peteet, Julia Albanesi; Creative Director, Tim McClure, GSD&M, Austin.
▼

Product brochure for the Wingate Collection of traditional desks, chairs and casegoods, manufactured by Novikoff, Inc., Fort Worth. Designer, Don Sibley; Copywriter, Margie Bowles; Photographers, Klein & Wilson.
▼

Logo design for Lakeline Mall/Melvin Simon, Indiana. Designer, Julia Albanesi.
▶

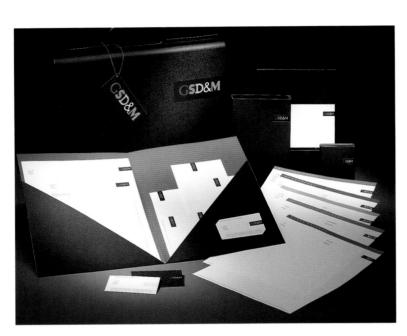

Logo design for Hammons Equestrian Center. Designer, Julia Albanesi.
◀

Logo design for Texas Association for Stolen Children (TASC). Designer, David Beck.
▲

Logo design for Polly Ellerman, fashion designer. Designer, Paul Black.
▶

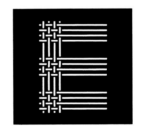

Mardi Gras Galveston poster designs for the Galveston Park Board, Galveston, Texas. Each poster in the series salutes the traditional carnival of a chosen country. Designers and Illustrators, Don Sibley (Venice), and Rex Peteet (Brazil).
▼

Logo design for Union Station, Washington, D.C./Lasalle Partners, Chicago. Designer, David Beck.
▶

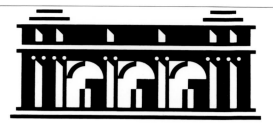

Capabilities brochure for Morris Architects, Houston. The client's 50 year history is presented in a time-line that is revealed at the front and back of the brochure. Designers, Rex Peteet and Paul Black; Copywriter, Paula Hewitt; various Photographers and Illustrators.
▼

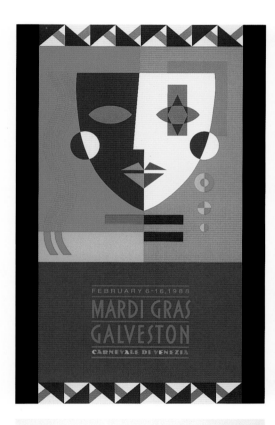

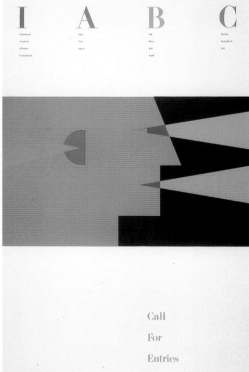

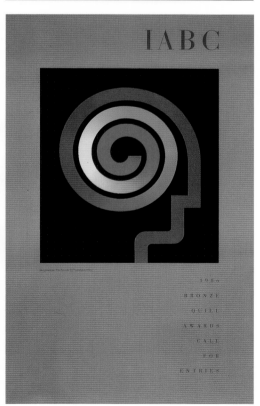

Call for Entries posters for International Association of Business Communicators, Dallas Chapter. Designers and Illustrators; Rex Peteet (1985), Don Sibley (1986).
◀

Sibley/Peteet Design, Inc.

Capabilities brochure for Trammell Crow Company, Dallas. The client is a premier international real estate developer. Designer, Don Sibley; Copywriter, Lee Herrick; Photographer, Joe Aker.
▶

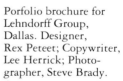

Poster announcement for the White Rock Marathon, Dallas. Designer and Illustrator, Rex Peteet.
▲

Capabilities brochure for Benson Hlavaty Architects, Dallas. The design includes a laser die-cut slipcase, portfolio, and various modular inserts. Designer and Copywriter, Don Sibley; Photographer, Burton Pritzker.
▶

Porfolio brochure for Lehndorff Group, Dallas. Designer, Rex Peteet; Copywriter, Lee Herrick; Photographer, Steve Brady.
▲

Logo design for Haggar
Apparel Company, Dallas.
Designer, Walter Horton.
▶

Go Van Gogh outreach
van for the Dallas
Museum of Art. The
van celebrates the 10th
anniversary of the
program, which brings
museum projects to
schools and retirement
facilities. Designer,
Rex Peteet; Illustration,
Sibley/ Peteet Design.
▼

Logo design for
KXTX Channel 39,
Dallas. Designer,
Walter Horton.
▶

Corporate membership
brochure for the Dallas
Museum of Art, Dallas.
Designers and
Illustrators, Rex Peteet
and Julia Albanesi;
Copywriter, Rex Peteet;
Various Photographers.
◀

Logo design for Brophy
Brothers Fish Market
and Restaurant, Boston.
Designer and Illustrator,
Don Sibley.
▼

Siebert Design Associates, Inc.

323 East 8th Street
Cincinnati, OH 45202
513/241-4550

Left to right (standing), David Carroll, Barb Raymond, Steve Siebert, Diane Sullivan, Jeff Fassnacht; front row (seated), Lisa Ballard, Lori Siebert of Siebert Design Associates.
▼

"City Shapes" edition of Printing By Design, Volume 1, a bound collection of posters for Sidney Printing Works, Cincinnati, Ohio. Designer, Lori Siebert; Photographer, Jeff Friedman.
◄

"A Private Peek at Cincinnati's Best" invitation design for The Contemporary Arts Center, Cincinnati, Ohio. Designers, Diane Sullivan, Lori Siebert.
▲

Jerry N. Uelsmann poster to promote a special presentation of the photographer's work for the American Society of Magazine Photographers (ASMP), Cincinnati, Ohio chapter. Designer, Lori Siebert; Photographer, Jerry N. Uelsmann.
◄

Principal:
Lori Siebert
Year Founded: 1987
Size of Firm: 8

Key Clients:
The Beckett Paper
Company,
The Cincinnati
Park Board,
CompuServe,
The Contemporary
Arts Center,
The Ensemble Theatre
of Cincinnati,
Formica Corporation,
Gradison & Company,
Hewlett-Packard,
HOW Magazine,
McDonald & Company,
Mercy Health System,
NCR Corporation,
Upjohn

Siebert Design Associates

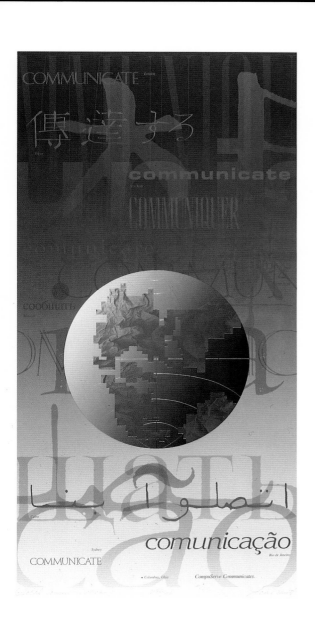

Poster design for
CompuServe, Columbus,
Ohio. Designers, David
Carroll, Lori Siebert, with
Sive Associates.

Siebert Design Associates. One of the beauties of starting a firm in Cincinnati, Ohio at a young age is that you don't know you are not supposed to take risks, to try approaches that are new and unique. Well, "How did you get away with that?" is the most often-asked question when viewing the Siebert Design Associates portfolio. They get away with it because what they don't risk is quality. Operating within a conservative market, how do you sell something unique? The key is collaboration. If the client feels like the ideas are half theirs, they are less likely to turn them down. Siebert designers really listen to their clients, and then intuitively interpret what the clients wish to communicate. They then create visual and verbal statements that are innovative, yet very logical. This innovation is not only evident in Siebert's approach, but also in their technique. The work of Siebert Design Associates is often fairly complex – layers of imagery and color, unusual folds and die-cuts – yet it is well organized. Although there is often a combination of color, texture, imagery, all elements work together within a common theme. They are uniquely able to make the complex simple.

Siebert Design Associates, Inc.

Folder design for Sound Images, Cincinnati, Ohio. The company writes and produces original music on sophisticated digital equipment. Designer, David Carroll.
▶

Formations new product campaign for Formica Corporation, Cincinnati, Ohio. The project consists of an outer folder that opens into a specification chart with seven single page die-cut inserts. Designers, Lori Siebert, Lisa Ballard.
▲

Annual reports for Mercy Health System, Cincinnati, Ohio. Designers, Lori Siebert, Barb Raymond, Lisa Ballard; Photographer, Gordon Morioka; Illustrator, Lisa Ballard.
▶

Identity and stationery system for Porter Printing, Inc., Cincinnati, Ohio. Designers, Lori Siebert, David Carroll.
▼

FINIS FINIS FINIS

Logo system for FINIS, Cincinnati, Ohio. Designers, Lori Siebert, Lisa Ballard; Illustrator, Lisa Ballard.
◀

Stationery system and Capabilities Brochure for FINIS, Cincinnati, Ohio. FINIS is a digital film/video post-production company. Designers and Illustrators, Lisa Ballard, Lori Siebert.
▼

Siebert Design Associates, Inc.

Notecard series for Good Nature Designs, Dayton, Ohio. Designers, Lori Siebert, Lisa Ballard, David Carroll, Barb Raymond. ▼

"Wild About the World" poster, notecards and stationery for Good Nature Designs, Dayton, Ohio. Designers, David Carroll, Lori Siebert. ▼

Identity system for Rags 2 Riches men's and women's apparel store. Designer, Lori Siebert, Dana Beverly; Illustrator, Dana Beverly; Photographer, Michael Wilson. ▼

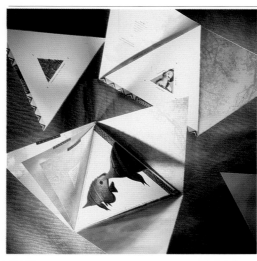

Concept "Triangle" promotion for The Beckett Paper Company, Hamilton, Ohio. The triangular shape relates to the three paper grade finishes and to the recycling symbol. Designer, Lori Siebert; Illustrators, Susan Naylor, Ron Bell.

◄

Siebert Design Associates, Inc.

Capabilities brochure for College Conservatory of Music, Cincinnati, Ohio. Each spread represents a division of the college. Designers, Lori Siebert, David Carroll.
▼

"Sleeping Beauty" poster for The Ensemble Theatre of Cincinnati, Cincinnati, Ohio; Designer, David Carroll; Illustrator, Susan Naylor.
▼

Poster designs for the Cincinnati Symphony and Pops Orchestras, Cincinnati, Ohio. Designer, Lori Siebert; Photonics/Digitized Imagery, Alan Brown.
▶

"Make Time for the Arts" calendar for Bowling Green State University, Bowling Green, Ohio. Each month's events are shown on the face of an oval. Dates move clockwise. Designer, Lori Siebert.
▼

Cover designs of TODAY Magazine for NCR Corporation, Dayton, Ohio. A new artist is featured on the cover each year. Illustrations depict issue themes. Designers, Lori Siebert, Lisa Ballard; Illustrators, Susan Naylor, Ron Bell, Leslie Cober.
▶

Subscription brochures for The Ensemble Theatre of Cincinnati. Designer, Lori Siebert; Photographer, Sandy Underwood; Illustrator, Susan Curtis.
◀

"The World Inside the Mysterious Black Squiggles" promotion for Gilbert Paper Company, Menasha, Wisconsin. The piece is about literacy. Four types of literature are presented—all run backwards on one spread and right reading on the next. Designer, Lori Siebert; Illustrators, Greg Dearth, David Sheldon; Photographers, Mark Alexander, Brad Smith.
▲

Rick Valicenti is principle and principal of the Chicago-based design firm THIRST. Father of two, husband, and friend.

A Few Minutes with Andy RudeKnee

Overheard and transcribed by Rick Valicenti

DESIGN. How come? What is design anyway? And who are these designers? Supposedly, they create everything: Perfume, couture, underwear, bedsheets, packaging, advertising, everything printed. But who really cares, anyway? And isn't everything more expensive when a designer gets involved? Who pays for it? You and I? Oh, I know, 'Value added.' 'The real difference.' 'The competitive edge.' 'Problem solving.' What problems do they solve anyhow? And who said they were qualified? Did you ever ask a designer to solve a problem? Maybe you've had a neighbor who was one. Was their yard nicer than yours? I suppose they had square shrubbery. Even an Italian car. Black for sure. Designers don't live in places we live. They must have special places to live. I wonder how they know where they are? Their homes have to be places designed by architects. Real ones. The ones who design all those dinner plates and tea kettles. Not the ones we hire for room additions. They're just friends of friends, anyhow. I overheard a bunch of designers once. At one of those charity events. I couldn't for the life of me get a handle on their gossip. They obviously care about different things than I do. I can usually follow just about anyone, but they're impossible. I guess it's because they care about details.

You know, "GOD is in details." One of the most famous designers said so. Mies somebody. Dead. Can't tell you what he designed. I always thought GOD was the best designer. My mother, bless her heart and soul, always said GOD stood for Greatest of Designers. "He must have been," she'd say, "'cause in seven days I can barely pick wallpaper for a bathroom let alone design the universe." Maybe Mom needed a designer. They probably do this stuff in their sleep. Pick colors, make symbols. What kind of person drew those signs on the bathrooms, anyhow? Women identified by a skirt. A designer, I suppose. But really now, do all women wear skirts? Did this symbol really capture the difference between the sexes? For everyone in the world? I wonder if a Scotsman ever went into the wrong bathroom?

If designers are so good at solving problems, how come we have so many problems? Not little ones, big ones! The kind that fill our evening news. Or do they just care about the commercials? Maybe that's the problem. The world probably needs a real designer to tell the rest of the designers to get with it. A designer I spoke to recently in San Francisco told me "two or more designers in a room are a bunch of pussies." What do you think he could be referring to anyway? It must be something under his skin because he seems really to care about details too. I'm told they even care about the space between letters. Is this a sickness or should I care about this? Maybe it's satisfying. It must be lucrative. Today's kids spend good money to study it in college. In fact, that must be the place they learn the answers to all those problems. How many problems could there be anyway? To me everything looks pretty much the same. That Nike swash looks like the one for Newport cigarettes. Do you think they're telling us something? AT&T's globe looks just like Minolta's. I can hardly keep up. My maga-zines, my kid's surfing magazines, movie posters, car ornaments, they all look pretty much the same to me. Even new cars all start looking pretty much the same after a while.

Maybe we're not supposed to know the difference. Unless I'm buying a new car I can barely tell the difference between a Japanese car and a new Chrysler. Could design be the real reason GM cars didn't sell? I guess most Americans can tell better than me because I always liked Cadillacs. Even when the fins disappeared. Remember when some designer in the '80s thought it would be fun to pretend the spare tire was attached to the lid of my trunk? I wonder where he got that idea? Or was it she? Was there a problem with us Cadillac owners, needing to be reassured that our car was carrying a spare tire? Or was this just some divine intervention in the shower? Do you think the designer got a bonus for this idea? I must admit, those GM and Ford cars of the late '50s were pretty cool. Why doesn't Ford just remake the '65 T-Bird and fire their designers? I'd buy it. Today's technology and the style to soothe my virility. I've always said, "My virility is my only weapon." Maybe that's why I'd never go into a bathroom identified with a skinny Pillsbury Doughboy wearing a skirt. And how come all designers seem young? I wonder what happens to old designers? They're probably in some Hall of Fame. Doesn't experience mean anything in that profession? Maybe the old designers quit 'cause they have no new problems to solve? Perhaps they hate changes as much as we do. Notice I said "we". Maybe they just stop caring. Boy, if that's the case, why should we care? Maybe they've learned something we don't know. Maybe it doesn't matter after all. You tell Madonna!

Right now it sure seems just the opposite: everywhere you look, everywhere you read, "So 'n so designed this," "design for the human race," "design makes a difference." You tell me, does it? It sure must. Ever see how many books come out each year on the subject? Seems like it's the most important thing since sliced bread. I opened one of those design annuals recently just to see what all the fuss was about. I was shocked. Birth announcements and annual reports. Do you think the chairman of IBM recommends that each of his grandchildren have a designed birth announcement? Maybe he asks his annual report designer to just do it. Seems like a modern thing to do. Back to those annuals. Who picks the designers to be included? I don't! But really, how come there's no copy, just credits? And only pictures of open books and business cards. I wonder if there's really just nothing to say! Or maybe designers who buy the books already know the story and want to keep it a secret from the rest of us. That they surely do, 'cause I still don't get it. In fact, it must be some perverse cult thing. I wonder what the initiation is. Can anyone join?

Come to think of it, I do owe those design types a debt of gratitude. For the Chicago Bulls' insignia, if nothing else. Do all champions have neat insignias? Not the Blue Jays, that's for sure. On Sundays, while I'm checkin' out the sports page, my wife's cutting coupons. Who makes her like to do that stuff anyway? Probably some designer. Mind control. It's just gotta be, it can't just be saving 25 cents. If it's mind control, that explains why their books have no copy. It's A BIG FAT SECRET. What do they know about me that I don't know? It's scary just to think about it. Maybe we're being manipulated. Must be happening to everyone. Can't just be me, can it? Do you think a little old-fashioned manipulation is OK, just as long as we're not being had? Gee, I wonder what the difference is? That's the big question anyhow, huh? If design makes a difference, what's the DIFFERENCE?

**Clifford Stoltze
Design**

49 Melcher Street
Boston, MA 02210
617/350-7109

Direct mail promotion
for Envision, Boston,
Massachusetts. A series
of cards were sent out a
week apart that spelled
out the name of the
company. Art Director
and Designer, Clifford
Stoltze; Designers,
Yin Yin Wong, Martin
Sorger.
▶

Posada/Procesión
Navdeña poster
design for the Institute
of Contemporary Art,
Boston, Massachusetts.
Designer, Clifford
Stoltze.
▼

Clifford Stoltze,
Principal of Clifford
Stoltze Design.
▲

The Institute of Contemporary Art
in conjunction with The Boston Center for the Arts and the exhibition
El Corazón Sangrante / The Bleeding Heart
presents

POSADA / PROCESIÓN NAVIDEÑA

FREE / GRATIS

Sunday / Domingo

December 15

1991

PRIMERA PARADA
Institute of Contemporary Art
955 Boylston Street, Boston
2:00 p.m.

SEGUNDA PARADA
Centro Cultural Jorge Hernández
85 West Newton Street, Boston
3:00 p.m.

ÚLTIMA PARADA Y FIESTA
Cyclorama
Boston Center for the Arts
539 Tremont Street, Boston
4:00 p.m.
puertas abiertas a las tres

FIESTA NAVIDEÑA

de 4:00 – 7:00 p.m.

Mariachi Guadalajara

Ballet Folklorico "Xochipilli"

Teatro Escena Latina

Aguinaldos y Música Navideña Latino Americana

Parranda

Icon box and folder
for Interleaf, Waltham,
Massachusetts. Designed
as an alternative to a
three-ring binder, and
used at Interleaf User's
Conference. Art Directors,
Tim Hiltabiddle,
Clifford Stoltze; Designers,
Clifford Stoltze, Carol Sly,
Laurie Hill.
◀

Principal:
Clifford Stoltze
Year Founded: 1985
Size of Firm: 4
Key Clients:
American Council for
International Studies,
The American Institute of
Graphic Arts (AIGA),
The Art Institute
of Boston,
Chelsea Pictures,
Envision,
Fidelity Investments,
Harvard Law School,
Houghton Mifflin,
Interleaf,
Massachusetts Higher
Education Assistance
Corporation,
Northeastern University,
Phoenix Technologies,
Reynolds-DeWalt
Printing,
Society for Environmental
Graphic Design

Clifford Stoltze Design

Although Boston is conservative in comparison to other U.S. cities, it has an abundance of businesses looking for design that is as smart as it is fresh. Clifford Stoltze has both in abundance. The diversity of Clifford Stoltze Design speaks to an ability to produce appropriate yet unconventional solutions for a wide range of clients. Designing the lecture posters for AIGA/Boston was an opportunity for the studio to produce something as progressive as the new directions represented in the series. The results brought local and national attention to the firm. While that particular solution may not suit every CSD client, the design process is one from which they have all benefited. As Clifford Stoltze explains, "I meet the expectations of the client and audience first, and then go beyond to reach my own expectations." A strong commitment to sophisticated and dynamic typography is the thread that ties it all together. "I believe typography has the power to convey a message beyond the literal meaning of the words."

Brochure design for the Graduate School of Arts and Sciences, Northeastern University, Boston, Massachusetts. Creative Director, Pamela Geddis, Geddis Productions; Art Director, Clifford Stoltze; Designers, Robert Beerman, Clifford Stoltze. ▲

AIGA New Directions, Winter 89/90 poster design for AIGA/Boston, Boston, Massachusetts. When two posters are hung side by side, front and back, the full image is revealed. Designers, Clifford Stoltze, Terry Swack; Photographer, Larry Joubert. ▶

202 **Clifford Stoltze Design**

MHEAC Annual Report 1988, for the Massachusetts Higher Education Assistance Corporation, Boston, Massachusetts. Art Director, Clifford Stoltze; Designers, Clifford Stoltze, Andrea Schmit; Photographer, Stuart Rosner; Writer, Christopher Tilghman ▼

MHEAC Annual Report 1989, for the Massachusetts Higher Education Assistance Corporaton, Boston, Massachusetts. Art Director, Clifford Stoltze; Designers, Clifford Stoltze, Kyong Choe; Illustrator, Tim Carroll; Writer, Christopher Tilghman. ▼

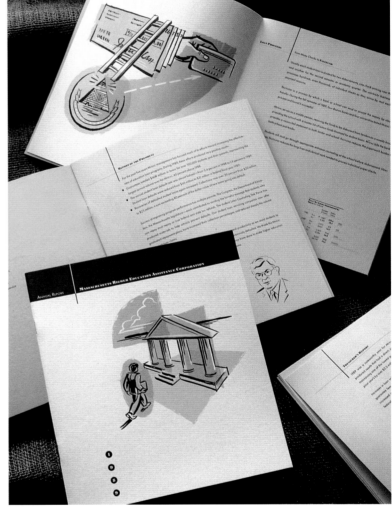

The series of annual reports for Massachusetts Higher Education Assistance Corporation is an excellent example of CSD's ability and willingness to make a project seem fresh year after year, proving it is not always necessary to change designers in order to achieve different results.

MHEAC Annual Report 1990, for the Massachusetts Higher Education Assistance Corporation, Boston, Massachusetts. Art Director, Clifford Stoltze; Designers, Clifford Stoltze, Robert Beerman, Laurie Hill; Photographers, Lucy Cobos, Frank Spinelli. ▶

MHEAC Annual Report 1991, for Massachusetts Higher Education Assistance Corporation, Boston, Massachusetts. Art Director, Clifford Stoltze; Designers, Clifford Stoltze, Pam Simonds; Photographer, Tom Wedell; Copy and Project Coordination, IDPR.
▼

Clifford Stoltze Design

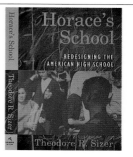

Horace's School, book jacket design for Houghton Mifflin, Boston, Massachusetts. Art Director, Michaela Sullivan; Designers, Clifford Stoltze, Robert Beerman; Photographer, Clifford Stoltze.
◄

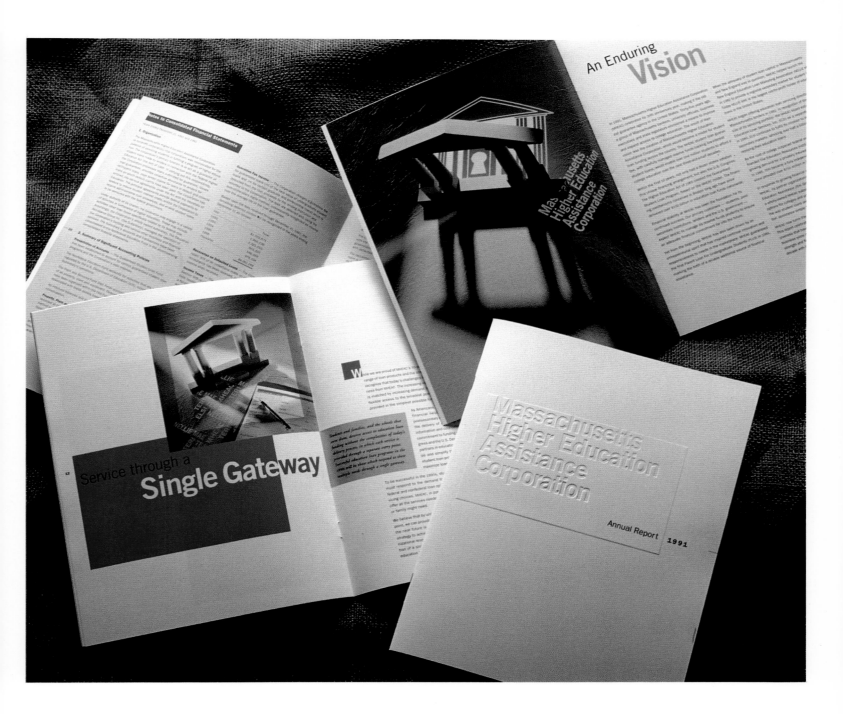

Logo design for Reynolds-DeWalt Printing, Inc., New Bedford, Massachusetts. Art Director, Julie Curtis Reed; Designer, Clifford Stoltze. ▶

Capabilities brochure/ promotion for Reynolds-DeWalt Printing, Inc., New Bedford, Massachusetts. Designer, Clifford Stoltze. ▼

Process Color Guide and presentation materials for Reynolds-DeWalt Printing, Inc., New Bedford, Massachusetts. Designer, Clifford Stoltze. ▲

Logo and graphic identity for Chelsea Pictures, Boston, New York, and Los Angeles. Art Director, Clifford Stoltze; Designers, Clifford Stoltze, Rick Stermole.
▼ ►

Greeting card design for Chelsea Pictures, Boston, Massachusetts. The logo was transformed into a winter greeting version. Art Director, Clifford Stoltze; Designer, Lisa Taft.
►

Promo sheet for Chelsea Pictures, Boston, Massachusetts. Art Director, Clifford Stoltze; Designer, Lisa Taft.
▼

Messages, journal of the Society for Enviromental Graphic Design, Boston, Massachusetts. Art Director and Designer, Clifford Stoltze; Designers, Robert Beerman, Rebecca Fagan.
►

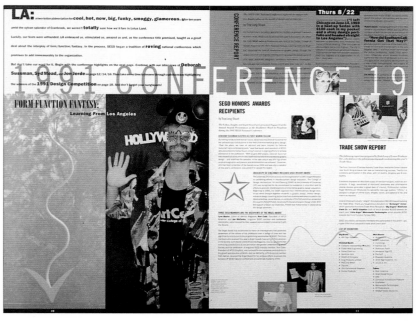

AIGA New Directions, Spring 89 poster design for AIGA/Boston, Boston, Massachusetts. Designers, Clifford Stoltze, Rick Stermole; Photographer, Stuart Darsh.
▼

Book jacket series for Eurasia Travel Guides for Houghton Mifflin, Boston, Massachusetts. Art Director, Sara Eisenman; Designer, Clifford Stoltze.
►

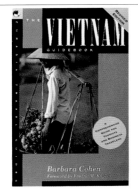
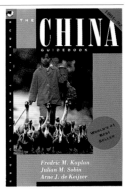

Not By Fact Alone, book jacket design for Houghton Mifflin, Boston, Massachusetts. Art Director, Sara Eisenman; Designer, Clifford Stoltze.
►

Raising the Roof, Opening Doors, poster design for City of Boston Public Facilities Department and the Boston Society of Architects. Designers, Clifford Stoltze, Rebecca Fagan; Photographers, Rebecca Fagan, Timothy Smith.
▲

**Clifford Stoltze
Design**

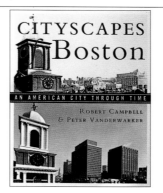

Cityscapes of Boston,
book jacket design
for Houghton Mifflin,
Boston, Massachusetts.
Art Director, Michaela
Sullivan; Designers,
Robert Beerman,
Clifford Stoltze.
◀

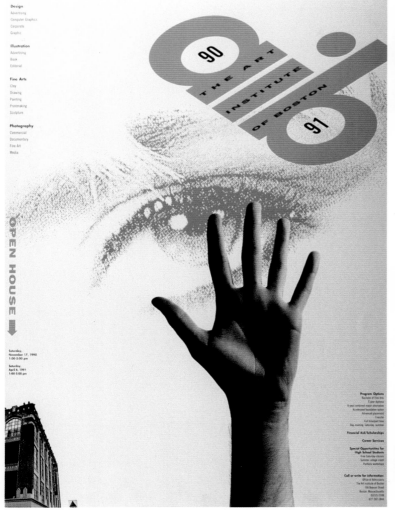

Catalog cover and
editorial spreads,
The Art Institute of
Boston 1990-91,
Boston, Massachusetts.
The catalog was an
opportunity to produce
an appropriately play-
ful and experimental
publication that broke
in all ways from the
typical college catalog
approach. Art Director,
Clifford Stoltze;
Designers, Clifford
Stoltze, Carol Sly,
Kyong Choe; Photog-
rapher, Richard Young;
Writer, Pamela Geddis.
▲ ▶

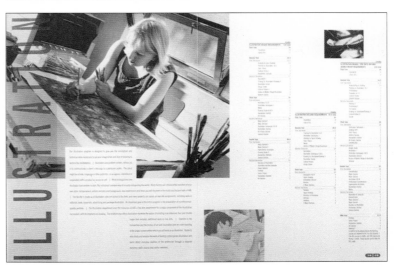

SullivanPerkins

2811 McKinney Avenue
Suite 320
Dallas, TX 75204
214/922-9080

Mark Perkins, left and
Ron Sullivan, principals
of SullivanPerkins.
▼

Signage system for
Riverwalk Market,
New Orleans, for The
Rouse Company.
▲ ▶

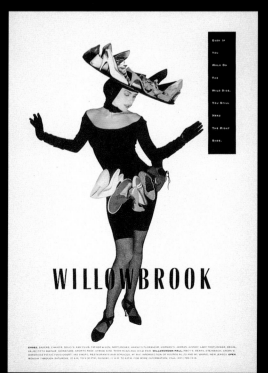

"Even if you walk on the
wild side, you still
need the right shoe," ad
for Willowbrook Mall,
Wayne, New Jersey,
for The Rouse Company.
◀

Principals:
Ron Sullivan
Mark Perkins
Year Founded: 1984
Size of Firm: 15
Key Clients:
American Airlines,
CenterMark,
Commercial Metals,
GTE,
Hill Partners,
Intertrans,
Northern Telecom,
The Rouse Company,
SnyderGeneral

SullivanPerkins

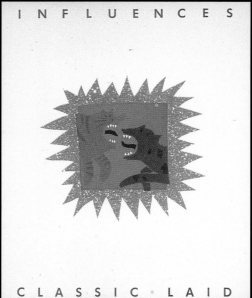

Influences," paper
promotion for Neenah
Paper, Atlanta, Georgia,
division of Kimberly-
Clark.
▲ ▶

SullivanPerkins is one of the largest independent creative groups in Texas. Of its current staff of 15, only three are in support services; the rest are either designers or writers, giving Sullivan Perkins an unusual amount of creative power to direct on behalf of its clients. The firm has no single sensibility; it respects the diversity of its clients. Provocative, appropriate design; smart, unclichéd writing; no formulas, nothing stamped out of a mold—these are the distinctions of the firm's best work. "You have to charm people with your work, you have to intrigue them. What you cannot do is confuse them. Clarity is paramount. We want everything we do to look great. But our work isn't about achieving a look, it's about sending a message," says Mark Perkins. SullivanPerkins' particular strengths are threefold: its annual reports and corporate publications tackle serious business themes with verve and intelligence; as designers of marketing pieces and graphics for shopping centers, the firm has achieved distinction with such unique marketplaces as South Street Seaport in New York City, Bayside in Miami, Harborplace in Baltimore, Union Station in St. Louis, Arizona Center in Phoenix, and Westlake in Seattle; and, in environmental graphics, SullivanPerkins has developed a broad portfolio of signage and identity projects throughout the country. Send a message they do; what their design communicates is the energy of different ideas which coalesce into a very singular graphic solution—the right one for the client.

American Airlines annual report design, for AMR Corporation, Fort Worth, Texas.

"On the Move with Cellular," promotional brochure for Northern Telecom, Dallas, Texas. ▼

Visual identity/logo for Satellite Research Network, for J.C. Penney, Dallas, Texas. The client conducts market research through a satellite communications system. ▶

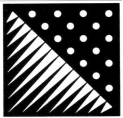

AMR CORPORATION 1990 ANNUAL REPORT

NORTHERN TELECOM CELLULAR SYSTEMS OVERVIEW

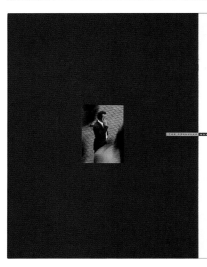

Promotional brochure
for The Selwyn School,
Denton, Texas.
▼

Logo system for
Southern Methodist
University graduate
business school,
Dallas, Texas.
▶

Annual report design
for Chapman Energy,
Dallas, Texas.
▼

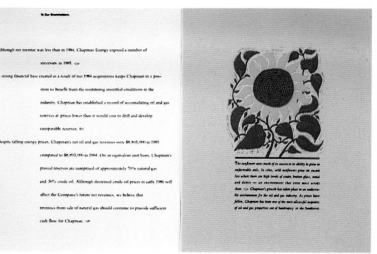

Shopping bag designs for North Star Mall, The Rouse Company, San Antonio, Texas.
▼

Remington Park logo design, for Lincoln Property Company, Dallas, Texas.
▶

REMINGTON
PARK

Thirty Year Anniversary bag for Cherry Hill Mall. The Rouse Company, Cherry Hill, New Jersey.
▶

"Your Guide to the Best of Times at South Street Seaport," invitation to opening, for South Street Seaport, The Rouse Company, New York, New York.
▶

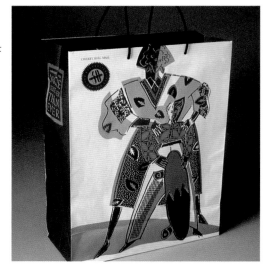

SullivanPerkins

Environmental graphics, interior display and signage program for Montgomery Mall, CenterMark, Bethesda, Maryland.
▼

Opening announcement of Bayside Marketplace, Miami, Florida.
▼

"Topanga to a T," invitation to kick off renovation of Topanga Plaza shopping center, Los Angeles, California.
▼

213

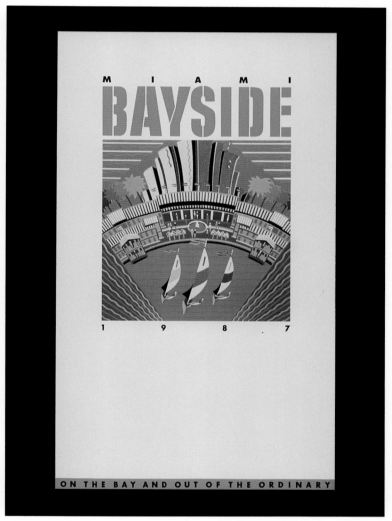

"Imagination" theme poster design/promotion for Harper House Color Separators, Dallas, Texas. The solution posed and answered the question "If 'Imagination' was a 'nation,' what kind of flag would it have?" ▼

Stationlines masthead design for newsletter of St. Louis Union Station, St. Louis, Missouri. The renovated train station is now a marketplace. ►

"Celebrating 50 Years in the Great American Marketplace," anniversary sweatshirt for The Rouse Company, Columbia, Maryland. ▲

Poster announcement of a speaker on the topic "How Atlanta Won the 1996 Olympic Bid," for the Dallas Society of Visual Communications, Dallas, Texas. ►

Invitation to design studios for the Chili Cook-Off, Dallas, Texas.
▼

Logo design for One Smart Cookie premium cookie store, for The Drexel Group, Dallas, Texas.
▶

Label and packaging design for Hogwash/Beefish pork and fish sauces, for HAM I AM, Dallas, Texas.
▼

SIXTH ANNUAL DESIGNERS CHILI COOKOFF

855 West Blackhawk
Chicago, IL 60622
312/951-5251

"Manhattan Gentle
Love" two in a series
of eight Valentine's
Day chocolates,
packages and logos for
Hontakasagoya, a
Japanese confectioner,
Osaka, Japan.
Designers, Rick
Valicenti, Tony
Klassen; Photography,
Tony Klassen.
▼

"Knowledge is Vision,"
from a series of personal
work. Designer and
Typographer, Rick
Valicenti; Photog-
raphers, Tony Klassen,
Rick Valicenti; Bronzo
type designed by Rick
Valicenti and Mouli
Marur.
▼

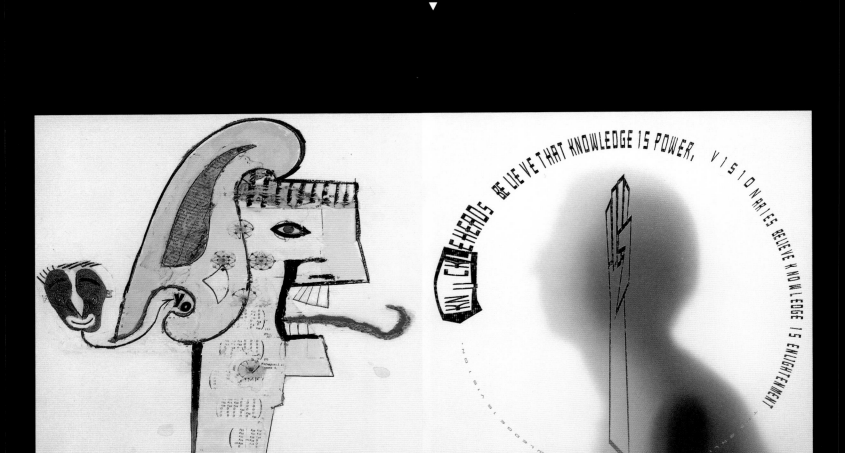

"False," one in a series of
10 letterpressed images in
the Principal Portfolio.
Designer, Rick Valicenti;
Letterpress, Julie Holcomb
Printers.
▼

Principal:
Rick Valicenti
Year Founded: 1982
Size of Firm: 9
Key Clients:
Cooper Lighting,
Gilbert Paper,
The Color Center,
Hontakasagoya (Osaka)

Thirst

Rick Valicenti, principal of Thirst, a design, photography and video collaborative, is devoted to creating Art with Function. "As we get closer to the millennium, civilization will rely on design to discover new ways that humans can communicate with one another. Ways that are free of anxiety and high on spirituality."

AMAZE, magazine ad promotion for Gilbert Paper, Menasha Wisconsin. Designer and Calligrapher, Rick Valicenti; Letterpress, Julie Holcomb Printers; Photographers, Corinne Pfister, Michael Pappas.
▼

Swatchbook for Legends Co., a Chicago clothing manufacturer. Designers, Rick Valicenti, Michael Giammanco.
◀

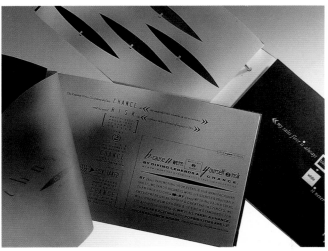

"Modernize," from the booklet "The 'Ize' Have It," for Gilbert Paper's Esse recycled paper promotion. Designer, Rick Valicenti; Photographers, Corinne Pfister, Michael Pappas; Hair and Makeup, Mark Stein.
▼

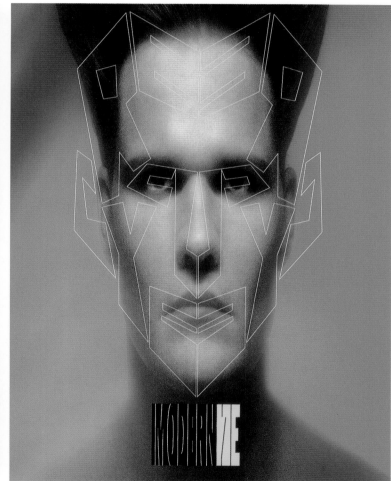

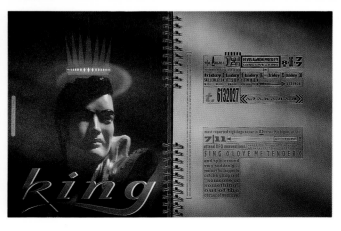

"The King and His Calendar," Esse paper promotion for Gilbert Paper, Menasha, Wisconsin. Designer, Rick Valicenti, Michael Giammanco; Photographers, Corinne Pfister, Michael Pappas.
◄

Cooper Lighting
Source catalog depicting
Cooper's showroom
headquarters, Elk
Grove Village, Illinois.
Designers, Rick
Valicenti, Michael
Giammanco; Photog-
raphers, Tom Vack,
Corinne Pfister.
▼

Emergency & Exit
Lighting catalog
and cover design, for
Cooper Lighting,
Elk Grove, Village,
Illinois. Designers,
Rick Valicenti, Richard
Weaver, Michael
Giammanco; Photog-
raphy, Kazu, François
Robert.
▼

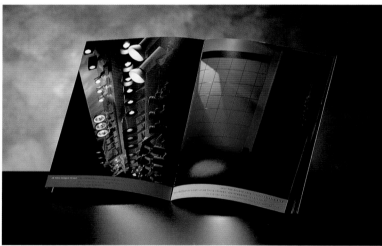

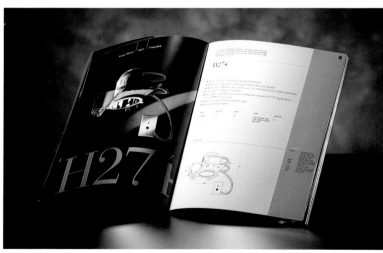

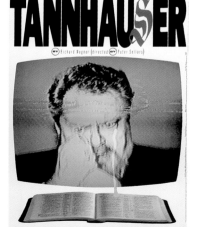

"Tannhauser," poster
design for the season
production of The Lyric
Opera of Chicago,
directed by Peter Sellars.
Designers, Rick
Valicenti, Peter Sellars;
Photography and Video
Imagery, Rick Valicenti,
Michael Giammanco.
◀

Axis identity program, developed for IDSA/Chicago Chapter exhibition of Chicago industrial design. Designers, Rick Valicenti, Tony Klassen; Photographer, Tad Takano.
▼

Thirst

A course catalogue for The Color Center-a collaboration between Scitex America Corp. and Thomas Munroe, Inc. Concept and Design, Rick Valicenti; Photography, Corinne Pfister and Michael Pappas; Digital Imaging, Tony Klassen; Typography, Richard Weaver.
▼

Identity designed for Yokohama Creation Square (YCS), a design-business-art incubation center created to enhance product and image development in the future. Designer, Rick Valicenti.
▼

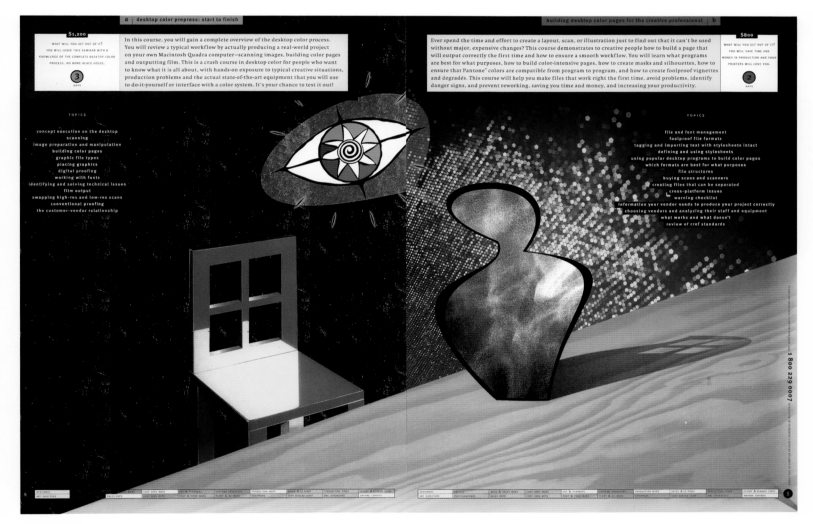

YOKOHAMA CREATION SQUARE

"We're not in it for the money," spread from Ear Magazine advertising a new jazz label, Ottava. Designers, Rick Valicenti, Tony Klassen; Joker/Bullet, Stock Photo.

▼

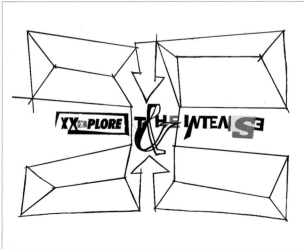

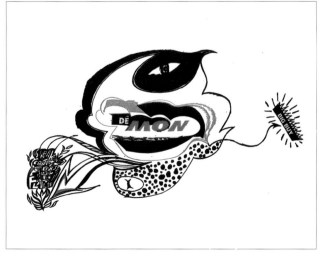

Two in a series of ten letterpressed typographic designs from the Killing Pretty Portfolio. Designer, Rick Valicenti; Letterpress, Julie Holcomb Printers.

◄

Poster announcing a
lecture series at University
of Pennsylvania, sponsored
by Details/Steelcase Design
Partnership. Illustrator,
Rick Valicenti.

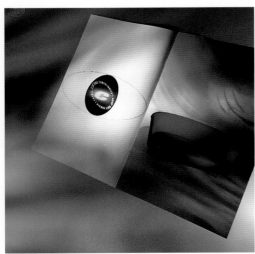

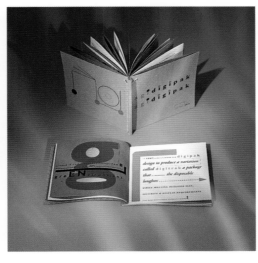

Light/Shadow, Centura
paper promotional
brochure for Consolidated
Papers, Chicago, Illinois.
Designers, Rick
Valicenti, Tony Klassen;
Photographers, Tom
Vack, Corinne Pfister.

AGI Digitimes #2,
promotional material
for AGI, Inc., Melrose
Park, Illinois. Designers,
Rick Valicenti, Michael
Giammanco; Photog-
raphy, Rick Valicenti,
Tony Klassen.

284 King Street East
Toronto, Ontario
CAN M5A 1K4
416/366-7100

Tudhope Associates'
logo. Art Directors,
Bev Tudhope, Ian
Tudhope; Designer,
Todd Richards.
◄

Bev Tudhope, left,
and Ian Tudhope,
principals of Tudhope
Associates Inc.
Photographer, Dan Lim.
▼

Tudhope Associates'
moving announcement.
The tails of the aircraft
are numbered with the
new east side address of
the firm. Art directors,

Bev Tudhope, Ian
Tudhope; Designer,
Todd Richards.
▲

Tudhope Associates'
self promotion. Art
Directors, Bev Tudhope,
Ian Tudhope; Designer,
Todd Richards; Photog-
rapher, Dan Lim.
▼

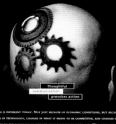

Pine cone holiday gift
for Tudhope clients
reflects environmental
as well as seasonal con-
notations. Art Directors,
Bev Tudhope, Ian
Tudhope; Designers
Todd Richards, Peggy
Rhodes.
▶

Tudhope Associates'
new office opening
party invitation. Art
Directors, Bev
Tudhope, Ian Tudhope;
Designer, Todd
Richards.
◄

Principals:
Bev Tudhope
Ian Tudhope
Year Founded: 1980
Size of Firm: 20
Key Clients:
Cadillac Fairview,
Canadian Tire,
CIBC,
John Labatt,
National Gallery of
Canada,
National Trust,
Noranda Forest,
Olympia & York,
Ontario Hydro,
Rogers Cantel,
Wood Gundy

Tudhope Associates

Toronto-based Tudhope Associates has, in the past ten years, cultivated a broad spectrum of clients in communication and design projects which couple a Modernist ethic with modern technology. Principals and brothers Bev and Ian Tudhope pioneered the use of computer-assisted design and production in North America, significantly reducing costs to clients in every area of communications and production management. The firm's mark is evident in corporate identity, annual reports, real estate marketing programs, capabilities brochures, and signage for such clients as Olympia & York, National Gallery of Canada, John Labatt, Rogers Cantel, and Noranda Forest. Every project, from a single pine cone sent as a holiday gift to clients to a complete wayfinding program for the National Gallery of Canada, communicates an immediate idea with clarity and graphic simplicity.

Tudhope Associates Inc.
office exterior and interior.
Architects Kuwabara Payne
McKenna Blumberg.
Photographer, Steven Evans.
◄

Bay Adelaide Centre advertising for Trizec Properties/ Markborough Properties. Art Director, Ian Tudhope; Designer, William Lam.
▼

Tudhope Associates

Logo design for MCA Concerts Canada. Art Director, Bev Tudhope; Designers, Chris Bonthron, Chris Pichler, Todd Richards.
►

Magazine advertisements touting the advantages of College Park, a Toronto office/ retail development, for Toronto College Park. Art Director, Bev Tudhope; Designer, Douglas Counter; Illustrator, Steven Guarnaccia.
▼

CIBC Development Corporation advertisment. Art Directors, Kelvin Browne, Ian Tudhope; Designer, Douglas Counter.
◄

Wood Gundy advertising. Art Director, Bev Tudhope; Designer, Todd Richards; Illustrator, Franklin Hammond.
◄

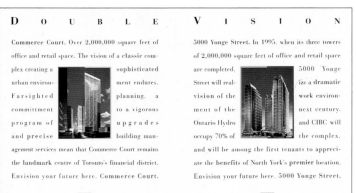

Rogers Cantel Mobile Communications 1991 annual report design. Art Director, Bev Tudhope; Designer, Yin Hoskins. ▼

King's Point logo for a waterfront condominium development. Art Director, Ian Tudhope; Designer, Chris Bonthron. ◄

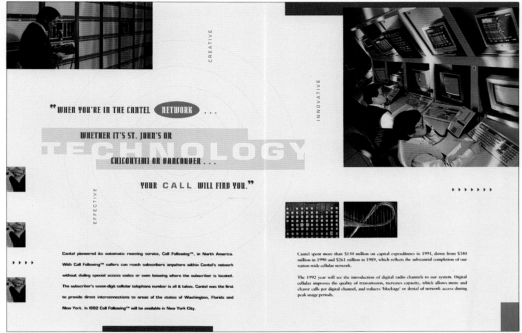

1989 annual report design for Trizec Corporation, Calgary. Art Director, Ian Tudhope; Designer, Chris Bonthron; Photographers, Wolfgang Hoyt, Hedrich Blessing. ◄

Noranda Forest 1991 annual report design, using 5 different paper stocks made by Noranda Forest, including cereal box board and brown kraft. Art Director, Bev Tudhope; Designer, Chris Bonthron; Illustrator, Valerie Sinclair. ◄

3-D full color direct mail promotion for One Liberty Plaza NYC. Art Director, Ian Tudhope; Designer, Yin Hoskins; Photographer, Wolfgang Hoyt.
▼

Tudhope Associates

Logo design for the 1989 Toronto Arts Awards. The logo can be reproduced in different colours and in two or three-dimensional iterations. Art Director, Ian Tudhope; Designers, Tammy Chaley, Yin Hoskins.
▼

Direct mail folder/poster promoting office space with roof garden at Olympia Centre, Chicago for Olympia & York. Art Director, Bev Tudhope; Designer, Todd Richards; Illustrator, Heather Graham.
▼

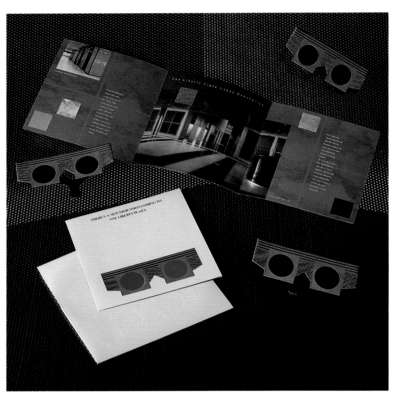

"Escape to the Wild" postcard/promotion for Desrosiers Dance Theatre. Art Director, Kelvin Browne; Designer and Photographer, Todd Richards.
◀

Poster designs promoting T-D Centre, a retail shopping concourse in Mies Van der Rohe office tower complex, for Cadillac Fairview, Toronto. Art Director, Kelvin Browne; Designer, Peggy Rhodes.
▼

Holiday greeting for Quadrangle Architects was mailed flat and assembled by recipient. Art Director, Bev Tudhope; Designer, Chris Pichler.
▼

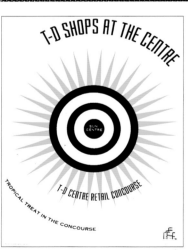

Logo design for National Trust Company. The motivational symbolism and colors were derived from consumer research results. Art Director, Bev Tudhope; Designer, John Spicer.
▶

Identity design for National Gallery of Canada, Ottawa allows print materials to be configured to suit a wide range of applications. Art Director, Ian Tudhope; Designers, Bob Boutilier, Bernard Stockl.
▼

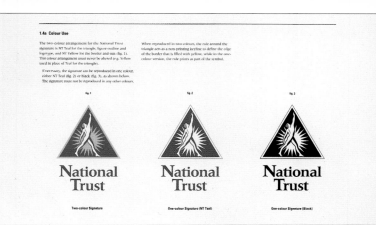

National Trust visual identity manual. Art Director, Bev Tudhope; Designer, Donna Gedeon.
▲

National Trust employee newsletter. Art Director, Bev Tudhope; Designer, Filip Jansky.
◀

Toronto-Dominion
Centre leasing brochure
for Cadillac Fairview,
Toronto, is a carefully
detailed minimalist
statement consistent
with the modernist
design of the Mies
Van der Rohe complex.
Art Director, Ian
Tudhope; Designers,
Douglas Counter,
Filip Jansky; Technical
Illustrator, Ian White;
Photographers, Steven
Evans, Jim Allen,
Hedrich Blessing.
▼

Bay Adelaide Centre
logo design for Trizec
Properties/Markborough
Properties. Art Director,
Ian Tudhope; Designer,
William Lam.
◄

Leasing brochure, 1325
Avenue of the Americas,
for Edward J. Minskoff
Equities, Inc., NYC.
Art Director, Ian
Tudhope; Designer,
Yin Hoskins; Photog-
raphers, Wolfgang Hoyt,
Hedrich Blessing,
Neal Slavin, Ron Baxter
Smith.
▼

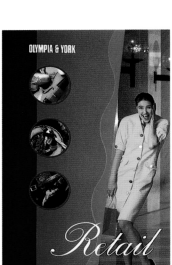

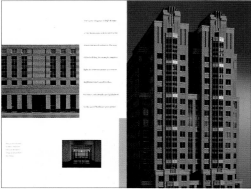

Retail leasing brochure
for Olympia & York
promotes the retail com-
ponent of the company's
major developments. Art
Director, Bev Tudhope;
Designer, Cathy Russell;
Photographers, Jim
Allen, Wolfgang Hoyt.
◄

Identity for Fusion Canada a division of Atomic Energy Canada. Art Director, Ian Tudhope; Designer, Don Dool.
▶

Identification and way-finding program for National Gallery of Canada, Ottawa. Art Director, Ian Tudhope; Designer, Michael Melnyk.
▼

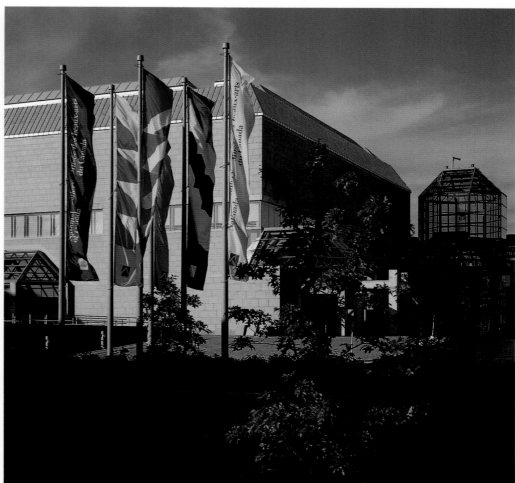

Olympia & York Display Gallery, NYC. Art Director, Bev Tudhope; Designer, Douglas Counter.
▲

National Gallery of Canada

Robert Valentine Incorporated

17 Vestry Street
New York, NY 10013
212/925-3103

Robert Valentine.
Principal, Robert
Valentine Incorporated.
▼

Letterhead design for
Robert Valentine
Incorporated, New York,
New York. Art Director
and Designer, Robert
Valentine; Photographer,
Maria Robledo.
◄

Brochure to launch
Aveda Natural Colour
Cosmetics, Minneapolis,
Minnesota. Art Director,
Robert Valentine;
Designers, Robert
Valentine, Dina
Dell'Arciprete, Kurt
Houser and Wayne
Wolf; Photographers,
Michael Thompson,
Kelly Stone and David
Sawyer.
►

p

Promotional brochure
and logo for Maria
Robledo Photography,
New York, New York.
Art Director, Robert
Valentine; Designers,
Robert Valentine and
Dina Dell'Arciprete;
Photographer, Maria
Robledo.
▼

Principal:
Robert Valentine
Year Founded: 1985
Size of Firm: 5
Key Clients:
Condé Nast Publications,
Crown Publishing
Group,
Gilbert Paper,
Carolyne Roehm, Inc.,
Time Warner,
Whitney Museum of
American Art,
Williams-Sonoma

Robert Valentine Incorporated

Robert Valentine believes that smart design comes as much from intuition as from intelligence. That feeling comes as much from common sense as from the heart. That honesty is the foundation of design and the measure of the designer. That without clarity and content, design fails to communicate. That style is not a solution, but a question answered by what a client needs. Smart design comes after hard work, tough decisions, and cold assessment. Its worth needn't be guessed; it proves itself. Where others see limits to design, Robert sees links. To broader areas of expertise. To pushing design's boundaries into other media. To exploring beyond expectations. Because when effort exceeds expectations, so does the outcome.

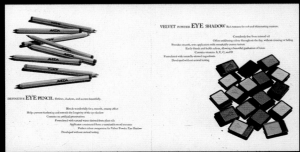

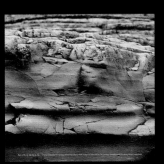

**Robert Valentine
Incorporated**

Moving announcement
for Authors and Artists
Group, New York,
New York. Art Director,
Robert Valentine;
Designers, Robert
Valentine and Wayne
Wolf; Illustrator, Eric
Hanson.
▼

Corporate identity for
Pottery Barn, a division
of Williams-Sonoma Inc.,
San Francisco, California.
Art Director, Robert
Valentine; Designers,
Robert Valentine and
Dina Dell'Arciprete.
►

1988 New Years shop-
ping bag and poster
for Bloomingdale's,
New York, New York.
Art Director, Robert
Valentine; Designers,
Robert Valentine and
Neville Brody.
▼

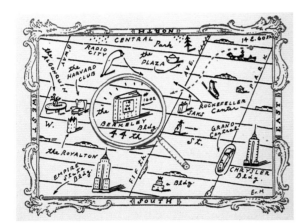

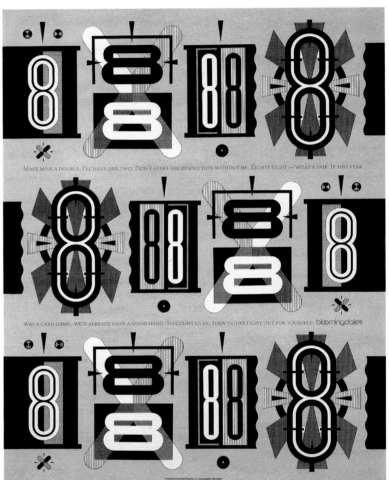

Robert Valentine Incorporated

Spain promotion for Bloomingdale's, New York, New York. Art Director and Designer, Robert Valentine; Illustrator, Sigfrido Martín Begué. ▼ ▶

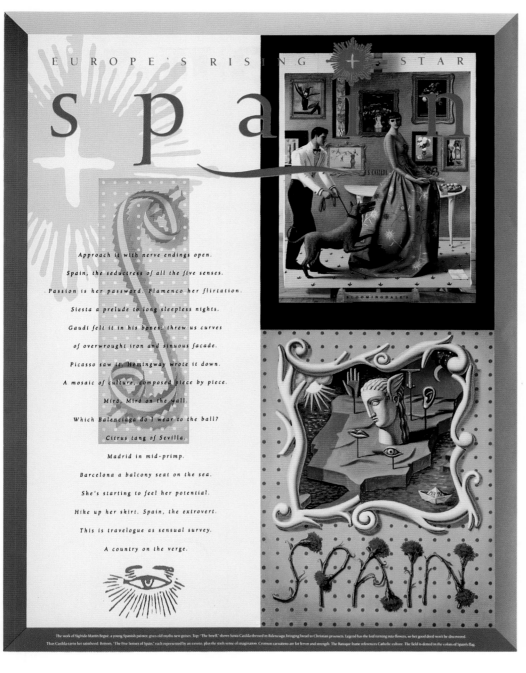

EUROPE'S RISING ✦ STAR

spain

Approach it with nerve endings open.

Spain, the seductress of all the five senses.

Passion is her password. Flamenco her flirtation.

Siesta a prelude to long sleepless nights.

Gaudí felt it in his bones; threw us curves

of overwrought iron and sinuous facade.

Picasso saw it. Hemingway wrote it down.

A mosaic of culture, composed piece by piece.

Miró, Miró on the wall.

Which Balenciaga do I wear to the ball?

Citrus tang of Sevilla.

Madrid in mid-primp.

Barcelona a balcony seat on the sea.

She's starting to feel her potential.

Hike up her skirt. Spain, the extrovert.

This is travelogue as sensual survey.

A country on the verge.

The work of Sigfrido Martín Begué, a young Spanish painter, gives old myths new guises. Top, "The Swell," shows Senta Casilda dressed in Balenciaga, bringing bread to Christian prisoners. Legend has the loaf turning into flowers, so her good deed won't be discovered. Thus Casilda earns her sainthood. Bottom, "The Five Senses of Spain," each represented by an icon, plus the sixth sense of imagination. Crimson carnations are for fervor and strength. The Baroque frame references Catholic culture. The field is dotted in the colors of Spain's flag.

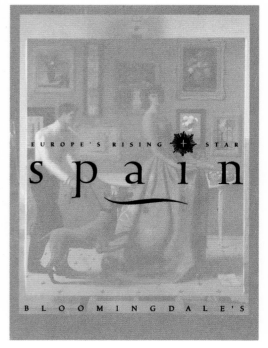

EUROPE'S RISING ✦ STAR

spain

BLOOMINGDALE'S

**Robert Valentine
Incorporated**

Image campaign
applications for Habitat
International, London,
England. Art Director
and Designer, Robert
Valentine; Photographer,
Maria Robledo.
▼ ▶

Series of trade ads for
Self Magazine. Art
Director and Designer,
Robert Valentine;
Designers, Robert
Valentine and Tracy
Brennan; Copywriters,
Shari Sims and Dean
Weller.
▲

Robert Valentine Incorporated

Spring and Summer 1991 catalogues for Habitat International. Art Director and Designer, Robert Valentine; Photographers, William Waldron and Maria Robledo. ▼

Logo design for "Fashion Follies," The Fashion Group International's Ninth Annual Night of Stars. Art Director and Designer, Robert Valentine; Illustrator, David Sheldon. ▼

Image brochure for launch of J.Crew in Japan. Creative Director, James Nevins, J.Crew Inc.; Art Director, Robert Valentine; Designers, Robert Valentine, Tracy Brennan and Dina Dell'Arciprete; Photographers, various. ▼

Robert Valentine Incorporated

Postcard and poster design for Imágenes de Mexico (Images of Mexico) promotional series which evolved from the original Un Libro en Imágenes promotion for Gilbert Paper, Menasha, Wisconsin. Art Director, Robert Valentine; Designers, Robert Valentine, Tracy Brennan; Photography, Craig Perman; Copywriter, Chuck Carlson. ▼

Book design of Un Libro en Imágenes (A Picture Book) promotion for Gilbert Paper. The book was the result of an unplanned creative exploration undertaken during Holy Week in Mexico. Art Director, Robert Valentine; Designers, Robert Valentine, Tracy Brennan; Photography, Craig Perman; Copywriter, Chuck Carlson. ▼

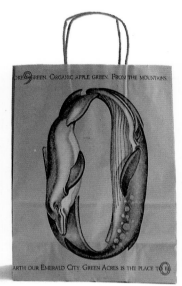

Vaughn Wedeen Creative, Inc.

407 Rio Grande NW
Albuquerque, NM 87104
505/243-4000

Steven Wedeen, Rick
Vaughn, and Richard
Kuhn, Principals
of Vaughn Wedeen
Creative, Inc.; Photog-
rapher, Michael Barley.
▼

Illustrations for
The Santa Fe Opera 1990
season were produced for
various applications.
Designer and Illustrator,
Rick Vaughn.
▲

Annual report design,
for Lasertechnics,
Albuquerque, New
Mexico. The client is a
high-tech laser company.
Designer, Steven
Wedeen; Photographer,
Michael Barley.
▶

Christmas self-promotional
gift crates, 1990. These
handmade wooden crates
include red chile jelly,
green chile salsa, and home-
baked blue corn tortillas.
Designers, Dan Flynn, Rick
Vaughn, Steven Wedeen;
Illustration, Gerhold/Smith
◀

Principals:
Rick Vaughn
Steven Wedeen
Richard Kuhn
Year Founded: 1982
Size of Firm: 13
Selected Key Clients:
Adolf Coors Company,
Champion International
Corp.,
Dion's Pizza,
Duke City Marathon,
Envision Utility
Software Corp.,
Foley's,
Gilbert Paper,
Horizon Heathcare Corp.,
Jones Intercable,
Lasertechnics,
Manville,
New Mexico Symphony
Orchestra,
Pecos River Learning
Centers,
Presbyterian Healthcare
Foundation,
QC Graphics,
Southwest Community
Health Services,
Tamarind Institute,
Taos Furniture,
The Cystic Fibrosis
Foundation,
The Santa Fe Opera,
U S WEST

Vaughn Wedeen Creative, Inc.

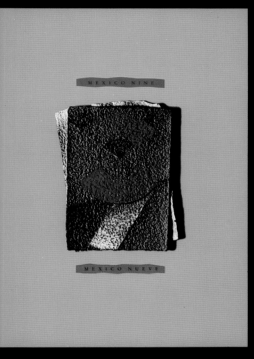

At Vaughn Wedeen Creative, Inc., passion and respect are the guiding principles of design. A passion for their work, and a respect for the power and importance of intelligent graphic design; a passion for their "enchanted" New Mexico environment, and a respect for their clients. Most of all, a respect for their audience: the "end users" of the myriad annual reports, sales brochures, identity systems, and commemorative posters that are part of the firm's consistently award-winning portfolio. Rick Vaughn left Dallas and Steve Wedeen escaped New York, to live among the beauty and lifestyle of the land they fell in love with. Armed with a passion for color and typography, words and pictures, and a stubborn refusal to believe you can't have it all, they proceeded to make an impact in graphic design from an unlikely location. They made their mark. And both principals continue to practice their passion. "Design has tremendous impact. Bad design insults our sensibilities. Good design entertains and communicates. Great design changes the way we look at our world and ourselves. Because we're no different from our audience. We are our audience."

Mexico Nine/Mexico Nueve book/catalog for the Tamarind Institute, Albuquerque, New Mexico. The book commemorates a two-year project in which nine Mexican artists were invited to produce lithographs at the Institute. Designer, Steven Wedeen.
▲

Illustration for The Santa Fe Opera 1990 season. Designer and Illustrator, Rick Vaughn.
▲

"Jack Can't Read," paper promotion/brochure for Gibert Paper, Menasha, Wisconsin. The problems of illiteracy were illustrated in the day-to-day struggles of one man. Designer and Writers, Steven Wedeen, Rick Vaughn, Gary Cascio, Richard Kuhn; Illustrator, Gary Cascio.
▶

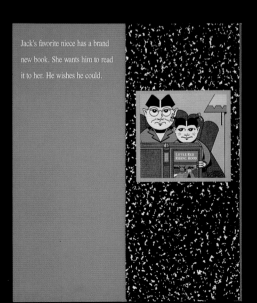

**Vaughn Wedeen
Creative, Inc.**

Catalog and identity for
Taos Furniture, Santa Fe,
New Mexico. Designer,
Rick Vaughn; Photog-
rapher, Robert Reck;
Stylist, David Moreno;
Writer, Richard Kuhn.
▼

"Ciao Down," poster for
a fundraising dinner
for the Cystic Fibrosis
Foundation, Albuquerque,
New Mexico. The Italian
theme was applied to
invitations, tickets, and
program book. Designer,
Steven Wedeen.
▲

"A Season of 'Classics,' "
brochure for the 1990-91
season of the New Mexico
Symphony Orchestra,
Albuquerque, New Mexico.
Designers, Steven Wedeen,
Dan Flynn.
▼

"A Few Choice Words,"
promotional brochure
for the New Mexico
Symphony Orchestra.
Designers, Steven
Wedeen, Dan Flynn.
▼

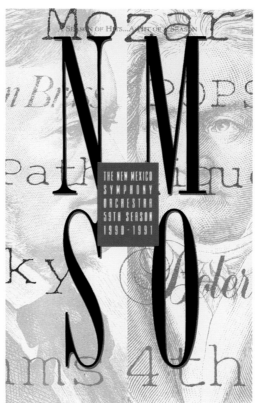

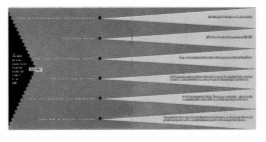

Vaughn Wedeen Creative, Inc.

"Are You In The Know?," direct mail promotional brochure and additional location announcement, for QC Graphics, Dallas, Texas. Designer, Rick Vaughn.
▼

Envision software brochure design and identity, for Envision Utility Software Corp., Santa Fe, New Mexico. Designer, Steven Wedeen; Photographer, Stephen Marks.
▼

Vaughn Wedeen Creative, Inc.

"Playing to Win" Workbook and Study Guide for Pecos River Learning Centers, a training and business education company, Santa Fe, New Mexico. Designer, Rick Vaughn; Illustrators, Jeff Koegel, Rick Vaughn; Writer, Richard Kuhn.
▼

"Taste", one of a series of posters illustrating the five senses, for Academy Printers, Albuquerque, New Mexico. Designer, Steven Wedeen; Illustrator, Mark Chamberlain.
▼

"The Whole Symphony Catalog," season brochure for the New Mexico Symphony Orchestra. Designers, Steven Wedeen, Dan Flynn; Photographer, Michael Barley.
▶

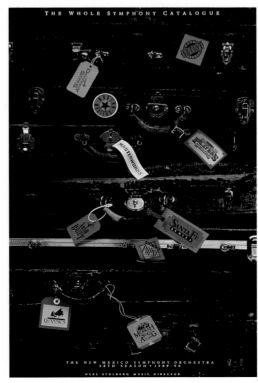

Vaughn Wedeen Creative, Inc.

"The Hunt for the Treasure of San Diego," sales campaign materials for U S WEST Communications, Phoenix, Arizona. Designers, Steven Wedeen, Lisa Graff; Illustration, Gerhold/Smith.
▼

Nearly 60 million Americans live and work in rural areas. But the economy in rural America continues to decline. Talents go unrecognized. Abilities go undeveloped. Dreams go unrealized. However, with some help and the right resources, this trend can be reversed.

"REVIVE', descriptive brochure inviting grant proposals designed to revitalize rural areas, for U S WEST Foundation, Denver, Colorado. Designer, Steven Wedeen; Photographers, Valerie Santagto, Elma Garcia, Don Getsug.
▲

**Vaughn Wedeen
Creative, Inc.**

"Mission: Possible," graphic identity system for U S WEST Communications, Phoenix, Arizona. An original typeface was created to establish an identity during pre-event mailings, without revealing the project "theme" before it took place. Designers, Steven Wedeen, Lisa Graff.
▼

U S WEST Report on Small Business, for U S WEST Communications, Phoenix, Arizona. Designer, Steven Wedeen; Illustrators, Douglas Smith, Jose Ortega, Melissa Grimes, Lonnie Sue Johnson, Curtis Parker, John Craig, Gerhold/Smith; Cover Photographer, Michael Barley.
▼

"Zoo Boo Three" Poster announcing a Halloween celebration at the Rio Grande Zoo. Albuquerque, New Mexico. Designer, Steven Wedeen.
▼

Index